Click, ***Bid***, **Collect.**

The Modern Guide to Online Art Buying

Simone Falanca

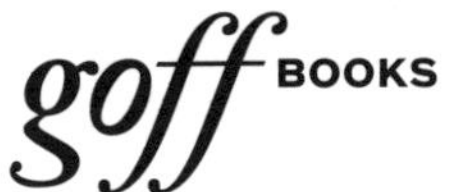

Art auctions are like a battlefield where collectors and dealers engage in a strategic dance, each maneuvering to claim their desired treasures amidst the cacophony of bids and the thrill of competition.

Marcel Proust

Commerce is a ruthless mistress, rewarding only those who dare to grasp her tightly.

Friedrich Nietzsche

In business, play the long game.

Meyer Lansky

Table of Contents

About the Author

Simone Falanca (1979) is an Italian author and investigative writer, currently based in Belgium, known for his incisive exploration of political and financial intrigue. He authored the book *Banche Armate alla Guerra: L'intrigo politico-finanziario dietro la guerra infinita* (2003), which critically examines the connections between financial institutions and military conflicts, shedding light on the political and financial complexities that drive global wars.

Falanca is also known for his work *Alfa e Beta: Cosa c'entrano Berlusconi e Dell'Utri con la stagione delle bombe 1992-93?* (2003) This book delves into the controversial links between prominent Italian political figures, including Silvio Berlusconi and Marcello Dell'Utri, and the series of bombings that shook Italy during 1992-1993. His writing is marked by a sharp, analytical style that seeks to uncover the hidden mechanisms of power and influence.

After publishing these works, he embarked on a corporate career that took him to live between Paris and Brussels. Recently, he has returned to the literary scene with a focus on the art world, writing about the art market and art collecting. Simone leverages his extensive experience to advise private clients on building their art collections, highlighting significant emerging and established artists.

He also manages a popular Instagram account, @auctionsinsider, where he shares insights into the world of art auctions, "one bid at a time."

Preface

Art has always been more than just an object of beauty for me—it is a visceral connection to the world, a medium through which we understand ourselves and others. In our shared human history, art has stood as a testament to our triumphs, our struggles, and the essence of what it means to be alive. Today, however, we find ourselves at a pivotal moment in the way we engage with art. The digital revolution has redefined how we experience creativity, placing the world's masterpieces, as well as the hidden gems of tomorrow's greats, at our fingertips. *Click, Bid, Collect*, is my response to that revolution—a call to action for anyone who believes in the transformative power of art and wants to claim their place in this brave new world of online art buying.

I wrote this book because I could feel the art world changing beneath my feet, and with it, the urgency to understand and engage with this new landscape.

This is about reclaiming the joy of discovery in an increasingly commercialized world, about finding your voice in the cacophony of options, and about connecting with art in ways that go beyond the transaction of money. This book is here to remind you that art is not merely something to be bought or sold, but something to be lived with, to be cherished, and to be explored.

My journey into the world of art didn't start in galleries or auction houses, but during a cold winter day when I was 10 years old. My father drove us through a five-hour snowstorm just to see a small 15th century sculpture, *Ilaria del Carretto*, in Lucca, Tuscany. At the time, I couldn't understand why he would go to such lengths, and I was honestly frustrated with him. But as we stood there, watching him gaze at the statue in awe, something quietly took root in me. It wasn't until many years later that I realized that moment had planted a seed; gradually, my own understanding of art began to flourish, and I came to appreciate it as something personal and deeply emotional.

Yet, as art moves further into the online world, that personal connection can sometimes feel distant, almost diminished. The overwhelming number of online platforms, the seemingly endless scroll of artworks, the constant buzz of bids and notifications—it's enough to make even the most seasoned collector feel lost. But I refuse to believe that this digital transformation has to strip art of its soul. In fact, I am convinced that the online art market holds incredible potential to democratize the art world, to make it more inclusive, and to bring the joy of collecting to people who never thought it was within their reach.

That is why I wrote *Click, Bid, Collect*—because now, more than ever, we need to navigate this new art world with passion, intention, and knowledge. The urgency to write this book stems from the realization that the rules of the game are changing, and fast. In this expanding digital marketplace, it's all too easy to be misled, to feel out of your depth, or worse, to lose the sense of wonder that should be at the heart of art buying. But I'm here to tell you that the magic is still there. The thrill of the hunt, the satisfaction of finding a piece that speaks to you, the joy of living with art that moves you—it's all possible, no matter where you are or what your budget might be.

Click, Bid, Collect is my way of showing you how to navigate this landscape with confidence. It is not just a guide to understanding the mechanics of online auctions or digital galleries, it's an invitation to dive in, to trust your instincts, and to rediscover what makes art so essential to our lives. I want this book to be your companion as you explore the possibilities, a resource that gives you the practical tools to make informed decisions, and a reminder that buying art is as much about heart as it is about strategy.

For far too long, the art world has been shrouded in an air of exclusivity, making many feel as though they don't belong unless they have millions to spend or insider knowledge passed down through generations. But that is no longer the case. The digital revolution has opened the door for anyone with curiosity and passion to become a collector. This is not just about buying art; it's about finding something that resonates with you, that speaks to your soul, and that fits into your life in a way that feels authentic.

I'm not interested in perpetuating the myth that art is only for the elite. I want to break that myth wide open. Art belongs to all of us. It's for the seasoned collector looking for their next masterpiece and for the person who has never bid on anything before in their life. It's for those who have always felt intimidated by the grandeur of galleries and for those who are excited to discover art from their living room. I wrote this book because I believe everyone deserves to experience the thrill of finding something that truly moves them, without feeling overwhelmed or out of place.

As I delved deeper into the world of online art buying, I realized how quickly this market was evolving. The traditional art world is scrambling to catch up, but the future is already here. Platforms like Saatchi Art, Artsy, and digital extensions of auction houses like Sotheby's have redefined the art landscape, and with the rise of artificial intelligence and blockchain, the way we buy and sell art is only going to keep changing. This book is about understanding these changes and using them to your advantage. It's about harnessing the power of technology while never losing sight of the reason we buy art in the first place—to bring something meaningful into our lives.

The urgency to write this book isn't just about keeping up with technological trends; it's about making sure that art, in all its forms, remains accessible, transparent, and full of wonder. It's about making sure that you feel empowered to participate in this ever-expanding market without losing sight of why art matters in the first place. Whether you're looking for a piece to invest in or simply want to find something beautiful to hang in your home, *Click, Bid, Collect* is here to guide you every step of the way.

In the pages that follow, you'll find practical advice, strategies, and insider tips to help you navigate this new world of online art buying. But more than that, I hope you'll find inspiration—a reminder that art is still about connection, about passion, and about finding beauty in unexpected places. This is your invitation to join the journey, to explore, to bid, to collect, and to fall in love with art all over again.

Acknowledgement

To Noémie, *ma femme*, without whom this book simply wouldn't exist. Her unwavering support, insight, and love have been my constant inspiration.

To my father, who instilled in me a love for art and its mysteries, sparking the curiosity that ultimately led me here.

1

Introduction

Welcome to the World of Online Art Buying: Where Creativity Meets Convenience

The art world has experienced a profound shift over the last few years, marked by the rapid expansion of the online art market. In 2023, online art sales reached an impressive $11 billion, reflecting a sustained surge compared to pre-pandemic levels in 2019, when sales were 85% lower. Although sales peaked in 2021 at $13.3 billion, the market has since stabilized, demonstrating that digital platforms for art transactions are here to stay, even as in-person auctions and gallery events have resumed.

The online art market has seen consistent growth, with experts projecting it will reach nearly $17.8 billion by 2030, fueled by a compound annual growth rate (CAGR) of 9%. This expansion is largely driven by the accessibility of online platforms like Artsy, Saatchi Art, Sotheby's digital marketplace and the hundreds of auctions houses worldwide, which have opened up new avenues for collectors and enthusiasts alike. These platforms not only democratize art buying by making it easier for a broader audience to participate, but they also provide a global stage for artists, giving them unprecedented reach.

I began writing this book during the COVID-19 pandemic, but the journey that led me here started much earlier. For years, I've appreciated art, gradually building a small, personal collection. Sometimes it was simply about picking up modest pieces that resonated with me. However, it wasn't until the world slowed down during the pandemic that I had the time to truly reflect on this passion.

As life paused, I found myself exploring the art market more deeply and thinking critically about my journey as a collector. This period of contemplation gave shape to the idea of writing this book. Inspired by my partner, a renowned art gallery owner, I also began to understand how the online art market was not only making art more accessible but also transforming the way we engage with and experience art.

My Personal Journey into the World of Art Buying

Transitioning from the corporate world to the art market wasn't just a shift in profession, it was a transformation of mindset. After years of rigid structures and predictable processes, I found the art world to be both exciting and intimidating. But with the support of my partner and a deepening sense of purpose, I embraced this new adventure.

It was during this time that I truly discovered the transformative power of art. Art wasn't just something beautiful to look at, it was a gateway to new ways of thinking, feeling, and understanding the world around me. I realized that buying art wasn't merely a financial transaction but a deeply personal experience. Each piece I encountered represented a story, a moment, a connection between the artist and myself.

With curiosity and a healthy dose of trepidation, I dove into the world of online art buying, eager to uncover its hidden treasures. I quickly learned that the online market offers incredible opportunities, but also challenges that require a blend of strategy, patience, and passion. It was through this journey of discovery that the idea for *Click, Bid, Collect* was born. This book is a reflection of the lessons I've learned, and it is written for anyone—whether you're a seasoned collector or someone just beginning their art-buying adventure.

Understanding the Online Art Market Landscape

Gone are the days of dusty galleries and stuffy auction houses. Today, the art world is just a click away, beckoning you to explore its boundless horizons from the comfort of your favorite armchair. Whether you're a seasoned collector seeking the next masterpiece to grace your walls or a curious novice dipping your toes into the waters of artistic expression, the online art market offers something for everyone.

Step into this digital wonderland and you'll find yourself spoiled for choice. From sleek, sophisticated marketplaces like Saatchi Art and Artsy to bustling auction houses such as Christie's and Sotheby's, the options are as diverse as the artworks themselves.

Yet, amid the proliferation of online marketplaces, it is platforms like Drouot Online and Interencheres Online that truly embody the spirit of the art market. Rooted in tradition yet embracing innovation, these platforms offer a glimpse into the world of auction houses, where the thrill of bidding and the excitement of discovery converge. In this book, we place a strong emphasis on the landscape of auction houses, recognizing their role as key players in the online art market. While galleries offer a curated selection of artworks, auction houses provide a comprehensive view of the market, with auctions spanning a wide range of categories and price points. By focusing on auction houses like Drouot Online, and Interencheres Online, readers gain insight into the dynamics of the art market and the opportunities available to collectors in the digital age.

Overview of Drouot Online and Interencheres Online

Ah, Paris—the city of lights, love, and legendary art. It's no wonder, then, that two of the most esteemed online platforms for art auctions hail from the heart of France. Let's delve deeper into the rich heritage and innovative offerings of Drouot Online and Interencheres Online, two giants in the digital art market that have revolutionized how we discover, appreciate, and acquire art.

Drouot Online and Interencheres Online represent significant advancements in the auction industry, leveraging digital platforms to enhance accessibility and reach. These platforms exemplify the evolution of traditional auction houses into the digital age, maintaining rigorous standards while expanding their global presence.

Drouot Online is the digital extension of Hôtel Drouot, established in 1852 in Paris. Hôtel Drouot has been a central venue for the auctioning of fine art, antiques, and collectibles, serving as a marketplace for collectors, dealers, and art enthusiasts globally. The institution's rich history and commitment to authenticity, provenance, and quality have solidified its status as a leading authority in the art market.

The transition to an online platform allows Drouot to extend its reach beyond its physical location. Drouot Online provides a comprehensive marketplace where users can explore a vast array of items, including fine art, decorative objects, rare books, and vintage wines. The platform offers a user-friendly interface with detailed listings and high-resolution images, facilitating confident browsing and bidding. Additionally, Drouot Online provides educational resources such as expert insights and historical context, aiding users in making informed decisions.

Founded in 2000, Interencheres Online connects over 200 French and international auction houses, offering a diverse range of items from various regions and categories. The platform highlights the richness of France's artistic heritage, featuring items from different locales, from Provence's landscapes to Paris's urban scenes.

Interencheres Online's strength lies in its ability to aggregate listings from numerous auction houses, providing a wide selection of fine art, antiques, collectibles, furniture, and jewelry. This diversity enables users to discover unique pieces that reflect France's cultural and artistic legacy. The platform's intuitive search functionality allows users to filter results by artist, category, price range, and auction house, making it easier to find specific items of interest. One of the significant advantages of Interencheres Online is its role in bridging local and global markets. It enables regional auction houses to reach a broader audience while giving international buyers' access to items that might otherwise be restricted to local markets. This democratization of access makes Interencheres a valuable resource for collectors and dealers worldwide.

Both Drouot Online and Interencheres Online exemplify how traditional auction houses can successfully transition into the digital age, offering unparalleled access to art and collectibles. They maintain the integrity and expertise of their storied pasts while embracing innovative technologies to reach a global audience. Whether you're a seasoned collector or a curious novice, these platforms invite you to explore, discover, and acquire pieces of history and beauty from the convenience of your own home. Through Drouot Online and Interencheres Online, the enchanting world of art auctions is more accessible and exciting than ever before.

Brace Yourself

Click, Bid, Collect is a declaration of empowerment—a recognition that every individual is entitled, if not to a Rembrandt, then to a genuine journey and hunt to find one's own artistic treasures. It is an acknowledgment that the true value of art lies not in its price tag or pedigree but in the personal connection and meaning it holds for the collector.

As we journey forth into the digital realms of art acquisition, let us remember the spirit of the hunter: the relentless pursuit of beauty, truth, and meaning in a world filled with wonders waiting to be discovered. Most importantly, as we wrap up this chapter, let's debunk the myth that the online art market is reserved solely for the deep-pocketed elite chasing after eye-watering masterpieces. No, no, my friend. It's a vibrant playground where art aficionados of all stripes can frolic, regardless of their budget.

Forget what you've heard about needing a hefty wallet to play in this arena. With prices starting as low as €50, the online art world welcomes everyone with open arms. It's like the ultimate equalizer—where art lovers from all walks of life can come together and indulge their passion without breaking the bank.

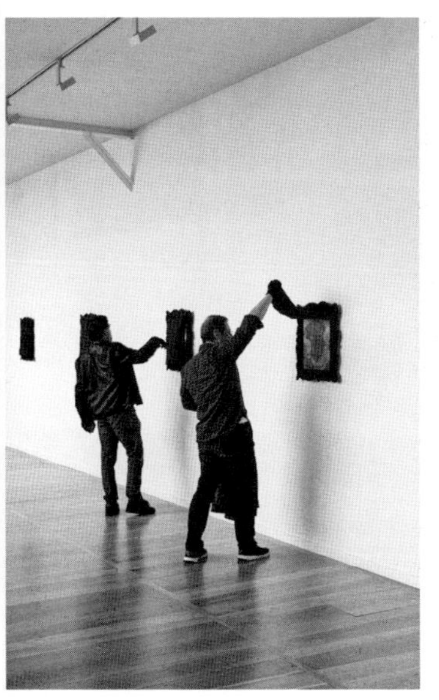

So, as we dive into the rest of this guide, remember: this isn't just for the fancy folks in penthouse suites—it's for us, the everyday art enthusiasts with a thirst for discovery. Whether you're a seasoned collector or a curious newbie, there's a treasure trove waiting for you in the digital art universe. So, let's strap on our virtual boots and embark on this exhilarating adventure together.

2 Getting Started

The first and most important step when buying art is to determine why you're buying it. Are you purchasing art for its decorative value to enhance the aesthetic appeal of your home or work environment? Or perhaps you have a deep appreciation for certain styles or artists and want to collect pieces as a hobby. Alternatively, are you approaching art as an investment? It might be a mix of some or all of these reasons.

If you're focused on beautifying a space, consider the environment where the artwork will be displayed. Pay attention not just to the colors in the room, but more importantly, to the lighting—both natural and artificial. If you have blank walls and aren't sure what will work, seek advice from artists or galleries. You may be surprised by how much can be achieved through the balance of complementary colors.

There are many online tools available, such as art visualizers that allow you to experiment with different artworks in your home or workplace. These tools help you visualize various sizes and placements of art, reducing the risk of making an expensive mistake. Another advantage of working with local artists is that many may offer the opportunity to view the art in your home before purchasing it.

For those looking for a temporary arrangement, galleries and artists often provide art rental services. This allows you to enjoy the beauty of a piece without committing long-term. Many rental schemes also offer discounts if you decide to purchase the artwork, making it easier to keep a piece you've fallen in love with.

Buy What you Like or Like What you Buy?

I can't fathom where the idea originated that one should purchase art they don't like, but it's a tenacious myth that needs to be rooted out. Many collectors and aspiring collectors hold the belief that in order to own valuable art, they must sometimes buy pieces they don't enjoy. It's astonishing how often I encounter collectors who have bought, or are considering buying—offline and online—art they don't actually appreciate; this notion is bizarre and completely misguided. A core principle of the art market is that if art is appreciated, it will likely appreciate in value. Common sense dictates that a painting sold in a market with high demand will fetch a better price. If you dislike a painting, it's likely that potential buyers will feel the same way.

Why buy solely based on an artist's name when there are so many beautiful and significant works available? There are plenty of important paintings that can fit various tastes and budgets.

"Good" doesn't have to mean "hard to appreciate." When you imagine a highly valuable artwork, it often is a piece of great beauty. For instance, Monet's multi-million-dollar water lily paintings are universally admired. Collectors should enjoy the art they purchase. The emotional and intellectual enrichment that art brings to our lives is what collecting is ultimately about. Art has the power to reveal who we are and to reflect the society we live in. Historical paintings can serve as documents of the past, illustrating where we have come from, while contemporary art can help us understand our current moment and envision our future. Art should engage and speak to the viewer. If your collection doesn't resonate with you, it's time for a change.

Collectors must form an emotional connection to their art to fully appreciate it. Those who are passionate about their collections tend to do better. I often find it refreshing when art dealers become so attached to pieces that they choose not to sell them. This deep connection to art differentiates true art lovers from mere traders. As a tip: observe what art dealers keep in their personal collections—they often retain the finest pieces. Superior art dealers trade art but also build personal collections.

The mindset of purchasing art based purely on potential financial gain, rather than enjoyment, indicates a persistent trend where collectors seek famous signatures rather than quality artworks. It's crucial never to buy art solely because of the artist's name; the piece itself must have intrinsic value. A bad painting by a renowned artist will always be a bad painting and will be treated as such in the market. Considering that the typical turnaround time for selling art can be ten years or more, it's a long wait to live with an artwork you don't love, bought solely for its perceived investment value.

The true value of an artwork is influenced by numerous subjective factors. The key to buying a quality piece with strong potential for capital growth is to evaluate it against a set of 'buying right' criteria. If an artwork meets or exceeds these criteria, the collector's risk is minimized.

Factors to consider when assessing an artwork's value include the artist's status—whether they are well-known or emerging. It's important to research and verify the artist's standing, rather than relying solely on the seller's claims.

Artists go through good and bad periods, influenced by various factors, including personal struggles. Understanding an artist's creative phases and why certain periods are more valued can guide collectors to focus on their best works.

Other crucial aspects include the artwork's medium, condition, provenance, and exhibition history. Size also matters—large contemporary pieces, for example, might not fit in standard residential spaces and could have limited appeal.

The subject matter of a painting should be broadly appealing and not overly niche or controversial. Unsigned works and those that frequently appear on the market can be less desirable. It's also wise to consider the broader art market and economic cycles: buy during downturns and sell during booms. Comparative value is essential; knowing the availability and prices of other works by the same artist can provide context for your purchase.

Finally, consider any additional costs like buyer's premiums, shipping, and insurance. Understanding the shifting trends and fashions in art can also inform your decisions, as artists and styles move in and out of favor over time. Acquiring works that express universal themes and emotions can offer both personal satisfaction and financial reward.

Setting Your Art Buying Goals

At the heart of any successful art-buying journey lies a clear understanding of your goals and aspirations as a collector. Take a moment to reflect on what draws you to the world of art and what you hope to achieve through your acquisitions. Are you looking to build a curated collection that reflects your personal taste and style? Are you seeking to invest in artworks with the potential for future appreciation? Or perhaps you're simply eager to surround yourself with pieces that evoke emotion and spark conversation.

By defining your art buying goals early on, you'll gain clarity and direction as you navigate the vast landscape of online art offerings. Consider factors such as your preferred artistic styles, mediums, and themes, as well as any specific artists or movements that resonate with you. Whether your vision is to create a cohesive collection around a central theme or to explore a diverse range of artistic expressions, articulating your goals will serve as a guiding light throughout your journey.

Comparing Art Mediums: Oils, Acrylics, Pastels, Prints, and Watercolors

Understanding the distinct characteristics of various art mediums is crucial for both artists and collectors. Each medium offers unique qualities in terms of color richness, texture, durability, and technique. Here's a comprehensive comparison of oils, acrylics, pastels, prints, and watercolors:

Oil Paints

Oil paints are known for their rich, vivid colors and remarkable flexibility. This medium uses pigment suspended in a vegetable-based oil, such as linseed oil. The high pigment concentration in oil paints allows for deeper, more intense hues compared to other mediums. The texture of oil paint can be manipulated extensively, providing opportunities for both thick, impasto applications and thin, delicate layers. Artists often use a variety of tools, including brushes, palette knives, and even their fingers to create diverse textures and effects.

One of the standout features of oil paints is their longevity. High-quality oil paintings, especially when executed on durable canvases or wooden panels, can endure for centuries. The oil medium's inherent properties, such as its ability to achieve a high gloss finish and its resistance to fading, make it a valuable investment for collectors. Historically, oils were produced using pigments that included toxic compounds like cobalt, cadmium, and zinc. However, modern advances have led to the development of safer, synthetic pigments that offer similar color intensity without environmental or health risks.

Acrylic Paints

Acrylic paints are a versatile, water-based medium that offers different properties compared to oils. Acrylics can be diluted with water, similar to watercolors, but they dry much faster—often within minutes to a few hours. This quick drying time can be advantageous for artists who prefer working in layers or need to complete their work in a shorter time frame. Once dried, acrylics form a durable, flexible layer that is less prone to cracking compared to oil paints.

Acrylics are also highly resistant to fading when sealed with a varnish or protective coating. Like oil paints, acrylics use pigments that are less likely to deteriorate under light exposure. This medium can mimic the appearance of oil paints or create effects unique to acrylics, such as vibrant color washes and smooth gradients. Although acrylics are generally considered less toxic than oils, it's still essential to use non-toxic, environmentally friendly paints and products.

Pastels

Pastels are a medium consisting of pure pigment mixed with a binder, often presented in stick form. Unlike paints, pastels do not require a drying process, as they are applied directly to paper or other surfaces. The color in pastels is exceptionally vivid due to the high concentration of pigment, providing a rich, almost luminous effect. The texture of pastels allows for blending and layering, making them suitable for both detailed and broad, expressive strokes.

Pastel artworks are generally less durable than oils or acrylics unless they are properly framed under glass or sealed with a fixative. Over time, pastels can be susceptible to smudging and fading, especially if exposed to direct light or handled frequently. Despite these limitations, pastels are cherished for their ability to produce strikingly vibrant and dynamic pieces with a unique texture.

Prints

Printmaking encompasses various techniques where an image is transferred from a matrix (such as a metal plate, wood block, or digital file) onto paper or other surfaces. Prints can range from traditional methods like etching and lithography to modern digital prints. The value of a print often depends on the edition size—limited editions are typically more valuable due to their scarcity.

Prints offer a different set of characteristics compared to paintings. They are usually less expensive and more accessible, allowing for wider distribution of an artist's work. However, prints generally lack the depth and texture of original paintings and can be more prone to fading over time if not properly preserved. High-quality prints are often created using archival inks and papers designed to resist fading and deterioration.

Watercolors

Watercolors are known for their delicate, translucent qualities and the ability to create both subtle and vibrant effects. This medium involves pigments suspended in a water-soluble binder, typically applied to specialized watercolor paper. The transparency of watercolors allows for layering, where lighter washes can be built up to achieve depth and detail. Despite their beauty, watercolors are generally less vivid compared to oils and acrylics due to their lighter pigmentation.

One of the primary concerns with watercolors is their susceptibility to fading. Over time, exposure to light and environmental factors can cause colors to lose their intensity. Nevertheless, skilled watercolorists can achieve remarkable vibrancy and richness through careful layering and technique. Watercolor paintings are often more affordable than oil or acrylic artworks, making them a popular choice for both new and seasoned collectors.

Each medium offers its own unique advantages and challenges, influencing the final appearance and longevity of the artwork. By understanding these differences, collectors and artists alike can make informed decisions that align with their aesthetic preferences and investment goals. Whether you're drawn to the rich textures of oil paints, the versatility of acrylics, the immediacy of pastels, the accessibility of prints, or the fluidity of watercolors, each medium provides a distinctive way to experience and enjoy art.

Other Examples of Acquisition-Goals:

1 · Discover a New Chagall: Imagine the exhilaration of unearthing the next Marc Chagall, an artist whose works will one day be revered and sought after by collectors worldwide. This pursuit requires a keen eye for talent and a willingness to take calculated risks on emerging artists. Begin by immersing yourself in local art scenes, visiting galleries and art fairs where new talents are showcased. Online platforms like Saatchi Art and Artsy can also be invaluable resources, offering access to a global network of emerging artists.

Investing in new artists is not just about the potential financial returns; it's also about supporting the creative process and fostering innovation within the art world. When you purchase a piece from an emerging artist, you're not only adding a unique work to your collection but also encouraging the artist to continue their journey. Establishing relationships with these artists early in their careers can be incredibly rewarding, providing you with insights into their creative processes and future works.

However, this approach does come with its challenges. Emerging artists often lack the extensive exhibition history and critical acclaim that more established artists have, making it essential to conduct thorough research. Look into their educational background, any awards or recognitions they've received and feedback from art critics and curators. Attend their exhibitions and speak with gallery owners to get a sense of their potential trajectory.

Despite the risks, the potential rewards of discovering a new Chagall are immense. Not only do you get to enjoy the beauty and originality of their early works, but you also have the opportunity to be part of their growth story. Imagine the pride and satisfaction of owning a piece from an artist who goes on to achieve great acclaim, knowing that you played a part in their journey.

2 · Rediscovering a Forgotten Artist: Embarking on the journey to rediscover a forgotten artist can be a deeply enriching experience, akin to a treasure hunt through the annals of art history. These artists, who may have been overlooked or forgotten, often have works of significant artistic value waiting to be rediscovered and appreciated anew. The process involves extensive research and a discerning eye to identify pieces that are not only aesthetically pleasing but also historically significant.

Start by delving into art historical records, auction databases, and old exhibition catalogues. Libraries and online archives can be invaluable resources for uncovering information about artists whose works have faded from public memory. Engaging with art historians, curators, and seasoned collectors can also provide insights and leads that are not easily accessible through conventional means.

Rediscovering a forgotten artist is not without its risks. The primary challenge lies in the limited market demand for their works. Unlike well-established names, these artists do not have an existing market base, making resale potentially difficult. Additionally, the authenticity and provenance of their works must be rigorously verified, as lesser-known artists are often targets for forgeries and misattributions.

Despite these challenges, the rewards can be substantial. By bringing attention to an overlooked talent, you contribute to the revival of their legacy and potentially increase the value of their works. The thrill of discovery, coupled with the satisfaction of restoring an artist's place in the art historical canon, is immensely gratifying. Moreover, owning a piece by a rediscovered artist adds a unique and personal dimension to your collection, distinguishing it from those focused solely on well-known names. Imagine uncovering a stunning painting by an artist who, though once celebrated, has since been forgotten. Through your efforts, their work gains recognition and appreciation, both aesthetically and monetarily. You not only own a beautiful piece of art but also become a steward of cultural heritage, playing a crucial role in the artist's posthumous recognition and success.

3 · The Misattributed Gem: In the annals of art history, there are numerous instances of artworks that have been misattributed or mistakenly overlooked, only to be rediscovered and recognized for their true worth years or even centuries later. One such example is the case of *The Card Players*, a series of paintings by French artist Paul Cézanne. Originally dismissed as mere studies or sketches, these works languished in obscurity for decades until art historians and experts reevaluated them and recognized their significance as masterpieces of modern art. Today, *The Card Players* is considered one of Cézanne's most important works, fetching astronomical prices at auction and garnering acclaim from collectors and scholars alike. For collectors with a keen eye and a willingness to delve into art history, the quest for misattributed masterpieces offers a tantalizing opportunity to acquire valuable artworks that have been overlooked or undervalued by the market. By conducting thorough research, consulting experts, and scrutinizing lesser-known works by renowned artists, collectors can uncover hidden gems that have the potential to yield significant returns and enrich their collections.

4 · Collecting Art for Emotional Connection: Sometimes, the most meaningful acquisitions are those that resonate with you on a deeply personal level. Whether it's a painting that transports you to a cherished memory or a sculpture that speaks to your soul, collecting art for emotional connection allows you to create a home filled with pieces that bring you joy and inspiration every day.

5 · Focusing on Art as an Investment: For those interested in art as an investment opportunity, strategic acquisitions based on market trends and historical performance can yield significant returns over time. Conduct thorough research, consult with art advisors, and stay informed about market developments to make informed decisions and maximize your investment potential.

Here are some modalities and websites that utilize data-driven approaches to aid in art buying:

Art Market Analysis Platforms: Platforms like Artnet and Artprice provide comprehensive market analysis, including price indices, auction results, and trend forecasts. These platforms leverage data analytics to offer insights into market dynamics, helping collectors make informed decisions about buying and selling artworks.

Art Investment Platforms: Investment platforms such as Masterworks and Maecenas enable investors to purchase shares in high-value artworks, effectively democratizing access to the art market. These platforms use data-driven algorithms to assess the investment potential of artworks and offer fractional ownership opportunities to investors.

Art Advisory Services: Art advisory firms like The Clarion List and The Art Gallerist utilize data analytics and market intelligence to offer personalized guidance to collectors. These firms analyze market trends, auction results, and artist performance metrics to advise clients on acquisitions, portfolio management, and investment strategies.

Online Auction Aggregators: Websites like Invaluable and LiveAuctioneers aggregate listings from various auction houses worldwide, allowing collectors to access a wide range of artworks and auction events in one platform. These platforms leverage data-driven algorithms to curate personalized recommendations and alerts based on users' preferences and interests.

Art Investment Funds: Investment funds such as Artemundi and The Fine Art Group pool investors' capital to acquire art assets with the aim of generating returns over time. These funds employ data-driven methodologies to assess risk, identify investment opportunities, and optimize portfolio performance in the art market.

Art investment funds have garnered attention in recent years as a novel way to access the art market without directly owning physical artworks. However, these funds remain a topic of debate and contention among investors and art enthusiasts alike. While they offer the potential for diversification and exposure to the art market's potential returns, many skeptics argue that the benefits may not yet outweigh the risks. Critics point to various challenges associated with art investment funds, including lack of transparency, high fees, and limited liquidity. Additionally, the subjective nature of valuing art and the unpredictable nature of the art market itself add layers of complexity and uncertainty to these investment vehicles. As such, investors are advised to approach art investment funds with caution and skepticism. While they may hold promise as part of a well-diversified investment portfolio, it's essential to very carefully weigh the potential benefits against the inherent risks. Ultimately, like any investment opportunity, art investment funds should be approached with a pinch of salt and careful consideration of one's financial goals and risk tolerance.

In the grand scheme of art buying, amidst all the talk of data-driven algorithms and expected returns, let me offer you a piece of personal advice: choose with your heart. Yes, you heard me right.

While it's tempting to get caught up in the numbers game, focusing on projected revenues and market trends, there's something infinitely more profound about falling in love with a piece of art. Picture this: waking up every morning to behold a painting or sculpture that speaks to your soul, that fills you with joy, that makes your heart skip a beat. That, my friend, is the true essence of art collecting.

So, when you're perusing galleries or scrolling through online auctions, don't just chase after the next big thing or the highest potential ROI. Instead, seek out artworks that resonate with you on a deep, visceral level. Choose pieces that stir something within you, that evoke emotions and memories that you simply can't imagine living without.

Whether your vision is to create a cohesive collection around a central theme or to explore a diverse range of artistic expressions, articulating your goals will serve as a guiding light throughout your journey.

Craft your vision—not necessarily carefully in the beginning—but start crafting it.

Researching Artists and Artworks

With your goals in mind, it's time to embark on a quest for artistic inspiration. Begin by immersing yourself in the rich tapestry of the art world, exploring the diverse array of artists, styles, and movements that shape our cultural landscape. Take advantage of online resources such as artist websites, galleries, and social media platforms to discover new talents and gain insights into their creative processes.

As you delve deeper into your research, pay close attention to the stories behind the artworks—the narratives, emotions, and ideas that inspired their creation. Engage with the art community, attend virtual exhibitions and artist talks, and participate in online forums and discussions to broaden your perspective and expand your horizons. Remember, the journey of art buying is as much about exploration and discovery as it is about acquisition, so embrace the opportunity to uncover hidden gems and forge meaningful connections with artists and fellow enthusiasts along the way.

The digital age has opened up a plethora of avenues for exploring the art world. Start by visiting artist websites, where you can often find detailed portfolios, artist statements, and even blogs or video content about their work. Websites like Artsy, Saatchi Art, and Behance offer platforms for artists to showcase their creations, making it easier for you to discover a variety of styles and mediums.

Social media platforms, particularly Instagram, have become invaluable tools for art discovery. Follow artists, galleries, and art fairs to stay updated on the latest trends and exhibitions. Instagram Stories and live sessions can provide behind-the-scenes looks at an artist's process, offering a more personal connection to their work. Don't hesitate to engage with artists by commenting on their posts or sending direct messages. Building a rapport with artists can offer deeper insights into their work and thought processes.

As you explore, pay attention to the narratives that accompany the artworks. Art is often a reflection of the artist's personal experiences, societal issues, or philosophical musings. These stories add depth and context, transforming a beautiful piece into a meaningful one. Read artist statements, exhibition reviews, and critical essays to understand the broader context of the work.

Consider the emotions and ideas conveyed through the art. A painting might capture the joy of a fleeting moment, the pain of a personal loss, or the complexities of identity and belonging. By understanding these emotional undercurrents, you can form a more intimate connection with the artwork.

Immersing yourself in the art world doesn't stop at passive observation. Actively engage with the community to enrich your experience. Virtual exhibitions and artist talks are excellent opportunities to hear directly from artists and curators. Platforms like Zoom and YouTube host numerous live and recorded sessions where you can learn about an artist's journey, their inspirations, and future projects.

Online forums and social media groups dedicated to art collecting and appreciation are also valuable resources. Websites like Reddit, Facebook, and specialized art forums offer spaces where you can discuss art, seek advice, and share your discoveries with like-minded individuals. Engaging in these communities can provide diverse perspectives and enhance your understanding of different art forms.

The process of researching and discovering art should be as enjoyable and fulfilling as the acquisition itself. Think of it as an adventure where every artist you discover and every story you learn adds to the richness of your journey. This exploratory phase allows you to develop your tastes and preferences, making your eventual purchases more meaningful.

One personal anecdote I cherish involves discovering an artist on Instagram who was relatively unknown but whose work resonated deeply with me. After following their progress and engaging with their posts, I decided to acquire one of their pieces. Not only did I end up with a beautiful artwork, but I also felt a genuine connection to the artist's journey and evolution.

Researching artists and artworks is a fundamental step in the art-buying process. Utilize the wealth of online resources available, immerse yourself in the stories behind the art, engage actively with the community, and embrace the journey of discovery. By doing so, you'll not only find pieces that resonate with you but also gain a deeper appreciation for the vibrant and diverse world of art.

3

Establishing Your Budget

The excitement of acquiring art, whether as an aesthetic addition to your space or as an investment, can be all-consuming. But behind the allure of beautiful pieces lies a critical necessity: approaching art buying with a clear financial strategy. Establishing a budget isn't just about ensuring you don't overspend, it's about creating a framework that allows for both passion and practicality, ensuring that the joy of collecting art can be sustained over the long term.

The art market, especially online, is rife with opportunities, but also with potential risks. Financial planning, therefore, becomes an essential tool for navigating this landscape successfully. In this chapter, we'll dive deep into the complexities of budgeting for art acquisitions, understanding both visible and hidden costs, and balancing emotional connection with financial prudence.

The Importance of Setting Financial Boundaries

Before making any decisions, the most critical step is determining why you're buying art. Is it for investment? To enhance your living or working space? Or perhaps you collect out of a deep appreciation for certain artists or styles? The answer to this question will guide the structure of your budget. While some may purchase art purely for its decorative appeal, others might view it as a way to diversify their financial portfolio, making the financial aspect more complex.

Art as an investment, for instance, requires a completely different budgeting approach compared to art bought for aesthetic pleasure. According to Clare McAndrew, an economist who specializes in the art market, collectors need to approach art buying with the same level of discipline as any other form of investment. Art can be a volatile market, and understanding its nuances—such as liquidity, market demand, and historical price trends—is vital for making sound financial decisions.

Assessing Your Financial Landscape

A critical first step is a full assessment of your financial position. This assessment should go beyond your bank balance and account for your broader financial landscape, which includes savings, investments, debts, and future financial obligations. Many financial advisors recommend using the 50-30-20 rule, a common budgeting principle where 50% of your income goes to essential expenses (housing, bills, groceries), 30% to discretionary spending (entertainment, travel, and in this case, art), and 20% to savings or investments.

Determine Your Disposable Income: Start by calculating your disposable income—the money left after covering all your essential expenses, like housing, food, transportation, and bills. This figure forms the base for determining how much you can comfortably allocate toward art acquisitions without dipping into savings or compromising your financial goals.

For example, if your disposable monthly income is $3,000, you may decide to allocate 10-15% ($300-$450) toward art. Over time, this fund accumulates and enables you to make larger purchases or spontaneous buys when an opportunity arises.

Set Aside Specific Funds: One effective strategy used by seasoned collectors is to create a separate art fund. Like saving for a home or a vacation, this fund is dedicated exclusively to art purchases. By setting aside a fixed percentage of your monthly income, you can save systematically for both larger, investment-grade artworks and more affordable, spontaneous purchases.

Long-Term Financial Planning: Consider your long-term savings and investments when determining your art budget. According to Deloitte's annual *Art & Finance Report*, art should form part of a diversified investment portfolio, with experts suggesting it represent no more than 10-15% of your overall investment strategy. This requires collaboration between your financial advisor and art advisors, particularly if you're buying art as a hedge against inflation or stock market volatility.

Understanding the Full Cost of Art Buying

The price tag on an artwork is just the beginning. When setting your budget, factor in additional costs such as:

Shipping Fees: These can vary widely depending on the size and weight of the artwork and the distance it needs to travel. International shipping can be particularly costly.

Taxes and Duties: Depending on your location and the origin of the artwork, you might have to pay import taxes or duties.

Transactional Expenses: These include payment processing fees, currency conversion fees if buying from international sellers, and potential insurance costs.

For instance, purchasing a painting for $500 might seem within your budget, but if shipping costs $150, taxes are $50, and insurance is another $30, the total expense quickly rises to $730.

Balancing Passion with Prudence

Striking the right balance between your love for art and financial responsibility is crucial. It's easy to get swept up in the excitement of an auction or the allure of a stunning piece. However, financial overextension can lead to stress and regret, which detracts from the joy of art collecting.

One strategy is to set a maximum limit for any single purchase and stick to it, no matter how tempting the art piece. For example, you might decide that no single artwork should exceed 20% of your annual art budget. If your yearly budget is $2,000, this means no artwork should cost more than $400.

Practical Tips and Personal Insights

Here are a few practical tips, infused with personal insights, to help you establish and adhere to your art-buying budget:

Create your own Art Fund: Similar to a vacation fund, set aside a specific amount of money each month for art purchases. This dedicated fund can help you manage your spending and save for more significant pieces over time.

Use Installment Plans: Some galleries and online platforms offer installment payment options. This can make higher-priced artworks more accessible without straining your finances all at once.

Seek Expert Advice: Engage with financial advisors who understand the art market. They can provide valuable insights into how art fits into your overall investment strategy and help you avoid common pitfalls.

Allow me to share a personal anecdote to illustrate the importance of budgeting in art buying. A few years ago, I came across a captivating piece by an emerging artist on Instagram. The artwork was priced at $1,200, which was beyond my immediate budget.

Instead of making an impulsive purchase, I contacted the artist and discussed a possible installment plan. We agreed on a payment schedule that allowed me to acquire the artwork without disrupting my financial stability. This experience not only brought a beautiful piece into my collection but also highlighted the importance of open communication and financial planning in art buying.

Establishing a budget is a critical step in the art-buying journey. By carefully assessing your financial situation, understanding the full cost of art acquisitions, and balancing your passion with prudence, you can enjoy the thrill of collecting art while maintaining financial health. Remember, the ultimate value of art lies in the joy, inspiration, and enrichment it brings to your life.

When Not to Buy Art

Collectors frequently seek advice on how and when to buy art, and sometimes even what specific pieces they should acquire. While it's crucial to understand the best practices for purchasing art, it's equally important to recognize red flags and situations to avoid. Knowing what to steer clear of is just as essential as knowing what to pursue.

One common mistake is making impulsive art purchases at night. This tendency is even more pronounced in the digital age, where online galleries and auctions are available around the clock. At night, your defenses are down, and you're more inclined to make decisions based on emotion rather than careful consideration. If you find an artwork online in the evening, save it to your favorites and revisit it the next day. This gives you the opportunity to reflect and research thoroughly before making a commitment.

Buying art while on vacation is another pitfall. With the rise of online platforms, it's easy to browse and purchase art from anywhere in the world, even while you're relaxing at a beach resort. However, holidays are meant for unwinding, not for making significant investment decisions. Many collectors have made hasty purchases during vacations, only to regret them later. It's better to wait until you're back home, in a familiar and focused environment, before finalizing any purchase.

Avoid buying art solely based on the artist's name. In the online world, it's easy to get swayed by big names and reputations. However, it's important to remember that you're purchasing the artwork itself, not just the name attached to it. Ensure that the piece resonates with you personally, beyond its creator's fame.

Be cautious of deals that seem too good to be true, especially online. If an online dealer drastically reduces the price of a piece, ask yourself why. It's crucial to investigate and understand the reasons behind such a discount before making a purchase.

Never buy art under pressure. Online auctions and flash sales often create a sense of urgency, pushing buyers to make quick decisions. It's essential to take your time, research thoroughly, and not let the ticking clock dictate your choices.

Think twice before purchasing art from non-traditional online venues like social media platforms. While Instagram and Facebook can showcase stunning artworks, it's best to buy from established online galleries and auction houses. This ensures that you're dealing with professionals who guarantee the quality and authenticity of the pieces.

Be wary of the excitement generated by opening nights or online launches. The art world, whether physical or digital, often involves a lot of hype, with virtual launch parties and influencer endorsements. This can lead to impulsive buys or bidding wars that inflate prices. Stay sober and level-headed, making decisions based on thorough research rather than the thrill of the moment.

Don't be fooled by red stickers or digital equivalents like "sold out" signs. This common practice can sometimes be a marketing ploy to create an illusion of popularity. Some online dealers might display these signs to make artworks appear in high demand. Resist the urge to be influenced solely by these visual cues.

In the digital age, these cautions extend to online art markets and virtual auctions. Platforms can create psychological pressures with limited-time offers and visually engaging interfaces designed to prompt quick decisions. Always take time to research, review high-resolution images, and read through detailed descriptions before making an online purchase. Use the same critical approach you would in a physical gallery to ensure your decisions are well-founded and reflect your true taste and interests. Moreover, verify the credibility of online sellers and check the provenance of artworks, especially those promoted through social media. The allure of beautifully curated online posts can sometimes mask the actual value and authenticity of the pieces.

4

Navigating Online Platforms

As the online art market continues to grow, finding the right platform to purchase art can be overwhelming. This chapter will provide a clear, practical guide to the various types of online art platforms, from virtual galleries to auction sites. We'll cover the essential features of each platform, offer tips for efficient browsing, and explain how to place bids effectively. With this knowledge, you'll be able to make informed choices and navigate the digital art landscape with ease.

Exploring Different Types of Online Art Platforms

The online art market encompasses a myriad of platforms, each offering its own unique selection of artworks, services, and experiences. From established marketplaces to specialized auction houses, the options are as diverse as the artworks themselves. Let's take a closer look at some of the most common types of online art platforms:

1 · **Marketplaces:** Online marketplaces like Saatchi Art, Artsy, and Etsy have democratized access to art, offering a vast array of pieces from a wide range of artists and galleries. These platforms are designed to be user-friendly, making it easy for buyers to browse, purchase, and even commission custom pieces.

Marketplaces curate their collections to provide a diverse selection of artworks, ranging from contemporary paintings and photography to sculpture and mixed media. This curation helps buyers discover new artists and trends, often through featured collections and artist spotlights. For instance, Saatchi Art's platform includes personalized recommendations and an art advisory service, offering tailored suggestions based on your preferences and budget.

Artsy connects collectors with artworks from leading galleries, art fairs, and auctions worldwide, encompassing both emerging and established artists. Its comprehensive database allows users to explore various art forms and movements, supported by extensive editorial content such as articles, interviews, and exhibition reviews. These resources enhance the buying experience by providing deeper insights into the art world, helping collectors make informed decisions.

Etsy, traditionally known for handmade crafts and vintage items, also serves as a vibrant marketplace for original artworks and prints. This platform is particularly advantageous for discovering unique and affordable pieces from independent artists and artisans. Direct communication with sellers on Etsy allows for customization and personal touches, creating a more intimate and engaging purchasing experience.

These marketplaces often feature advanced search filters, allowing collectors to narrow down options based on price, size, style, and color. The convenience of integrated payment systems, buyer protection policies, and customer reviews further enhances the transparency and trustworthiness of these platforms, making them appealing to both new and seasoned collectors.

2 · Auction Houses: The digital transformation has brought renowned auction houses like Christie's, Sotheby's, and Phillips into the online space, making the thrilling experience of competitive bidding more accessible. These platforms host regular online auctions featuring artworks from various styles, periods, and price points, offering collectors the chance to acquire coveted pieces from renowned artists and collections.

Participating in online auctions requires strategic planning and a thorough understanding of the auction process. Collectors must be aware of the "hammer price," which is the final bid amount accepted by the auctioneer, and the buyer's premium, an additional fee that can range from 15% to 25% of the hammer price. It is also essential to consider other associated costs such as shipping, taxes, and potential restoration fees.

The online platforms of these auction houses provide high-quality images, detailed descriptions, and provenance information, ensuring that buyers have all the necessary information to make informed decisions. Features such as real-time bidding updates, automated bidding systems, and virtual previews enhance the user experience, making it more interactive and engaging.

The strategic aspect of bidding involves setting a clear budget and adhering to it, despite the excitement and competitive nature of auctions. Successful bidding also requires understanding the rhythm of the auction, knowing when to place bids strategically, and staying calm under pressure to avoid overspending. Engaging with auction house specialists can provide valuable insights and advice, further enhancing the collector's confidence in their purchases.

3 · Specialized Platforms connecting Auctions Houses worldwide: Specialized platforms, such as Drouot Online and Interencheres Online, as anticipated in the 1st Chapter, play a pivotal role by connecting buyers with a vast array of auction houses, catering to niche markets and specific interests. These platforms focus on particular genres, mediums, or regions, offering a curated selection of items from reputable and vibrant auction houses and galleries around the world. Drouot Online, the digital extension of the prestigious Hôtel Drouot in Paris, provides access to a diverse range of items, from fine art and antiques to collectibles and jewelry. The platform's comprehensive catalogues, detailed descriptions, and high-quality images ensure that buyers have all the necessary information to make informed decisions. Interencheres Online connects over 300 French and international auction houses, offering a wide variety of artworks and collectibles. The platform's advanced search filters and detailed auction catalogues make it easy to find specific items of interest. These specialized platforms are particularly advantageous for collectors seeking rare or unique pieces that may not be available on broader marketplaces or larger auction houses.

4 · Direct-from-Artist Platforms: Direct-from-artist platforms such as Patreon and Buy Me A Coffee offer a unique and personal approach to art collecting by allowing buyers to support individual artists directly. These platforms foster closer connections between artists and collectors, providing a more engaging and rewarding experience. Patreon enables artists to offer tiered memberships, giving supporters access to exclusive content, early releases, and behind-the-scenes insights. Many artists also offer original artworks and prints as rewards for higher-tier patrons, creating a unique and rewarding experience for collectors. Buy Me A Coffee allows artists to receive support from fans through one-time donations or memberships, offering digital downloads, original artworks, and personalized messages as rewards. Supporting artists directly through these platforms not only provides financial backing but also builds a personal connection that enhances the collecting experience. By exploring the diverse range of online art platforms available, you'll gain insights into the different buying experiences and opportunities they offer, allowing you to find the platform that best aligns with your preferences and objectives.

Navigating the diverse landscape of online art platforms can be both exhilarating and daunting. A few years ago, I discovered a remarkable piece by an emerging digital artist on Artsy. The artist's unique blend of traditional painting techniques and digital manipulation fascinated me. After purchasing the artwork,

I reached out to the artist through Instagram to express my admiration. This led to a meaningful exchange of ideas and eventually a commissioned piece that perfectly matched my vision.

On another occasion, I participated in a live auction on Sotheby's online platform. The piece I was interested in was a mid-century abstract painting by a relatively unknown artist. I set a clear budget and monitored the auction closely. The adrenaline rush of the final bidding moments was exhilarating. As the bids soared higher and higher, I found myself at the edge of my seat, fingers poised over the bid button.

Then, as the price crept uncomfortably close to my upper limit, I had to make a choice: follow my heart or stick to my guns. My self-control kicked in just in time, and I let the final bid pass without clicking. The painting went to another bidder, but I kept my dignity—and my budget—intact. I like to think of it as a victory of wisdom over impulse, a testament to the importance of setting limits and knowing when to walk away. After all, there's always another piece out there, and sometimes, not winning is the best win of all.

How an Auction House Works

Auction houses are complex organizations designed to facilitate the sale of art, antiques, and collectibles to the highest bidder. These institutions play a pivotal role in the art market, acting as intermediaries between sellers and buyers. To understand their operation, it is essential to explore their structure, the roles of various employees, and their overarching interests.

Structure and Interests

The primary interest of an auction house is to maximize the sale price of items consigned to them, as they typically earn a commission based on the final hammer price. This commission, known as the buyer's premium, is an additional fee charged to the buyer on top of the hammer price. Auction houses also charge sellers a consignor's commission for handling their items, thus earning from both ends of the transaction.

Auction houses are structured to support this goal through a hierarchical organization that includes several specialized departments. These departments ensure the smooth operation of auctions and the proper handling of consigned items.

Key Roles and Employees

1 · Specialists and Experts: Specialists are experts in specific categories such as fine art, jewelry, antiques, or rare books. They are responsible for evaluating and authenticating items, determining their provenance, and providing estimates of their value. Their expertise ensures that items are accurately described and appraised.

2 · Consignment Managers: These professionals work with sellers to consign items to the auction house. They handle contracts, arrange for the transportation and storage of items, and ensure that all necessary documentation is in order. They act as the primary liaison between the auction house and the consignor.

3 · Cataloguers: Cataloguers create detailed descriptions of the items to be auctioned, which are published in the auction catalogue. These descriptions include information about the item's provenance, condition, and estimated value. The catalogue serves as a critical tool for potential buyers to assess the items before the auction.

4 · Marketing and Communications Teams: These teams are responsible for promoting upcoming auctions. They create marketing campaigns, manage public relations, and engage with potential buyers through various channels, including social media, email newsletters, and print advertisements. Their goal is to attract as many bidders as possible to maximize auction results.

5 · Auctioneers: Auctioneers are the public face of the auction house during the sale. They conduct the auction, manage the bidding process, and ensure that the auction runs smoothly and efficiently. Skilled auctioneers can drive higher bids through their performance and interaction with the bidders.

6 · Client Services: This team handles inquiries from potential buyers, assists with registration for the auction, and provides customer service throughout the process. They ensure that buyers have a positive experience and are informed about the auction procedures.

7 · Operations and Logistics: This department manages the physical aspects of the auction, including the storage, transportation, and display of items. They ensure that items are handled securely and presented attractively during pre-auction exhibitions and the auction itself.

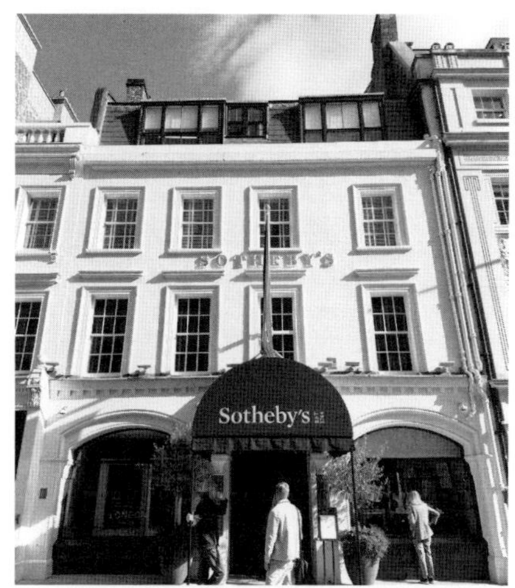

8 · Finance and Legal Teams: These teams handle the financial transactions and legal aspects of the auction process. They ensure that all sales are completed legally and ethically, manage payments, and address any legal issues that may arise.

Auction houses operate as well-oiled machines, combining the expertise of various professionals to facilitate the sale of valuable items. By understanding their structure and roles, collectors and consignors can better navigate the auction process and appreciate the intricate workings of these institutions.

Tips for Browsing and Searching Effectively

Once you've familiarized yourself with the various online art platforms, it's time to roll up your sleeves and start exploring. Here are some tips for browsing and searching effectively:

1 · Use Filters and Categories: Most online platforms offer filters and categories to help narrow down your search. Use these tools to refine your search by criteria such as artist, style, medium, size, and price range.

Refine by Medium and Style: Start by narrowing down your search based on the medium and style of artwork you prefer. For example, if you're drawn to oil paintings, you can filter your search to display only artworks created with this medium. Similarly, if you have a penchant for abstract art, you can refine your search to show artworks that fall within this stylistic category. For example: suppose you're searching for a statement piece to adorn your living room. By filtering your search to display large-scale oil paintings in the abstract expressionist style, you can quickly narrow down your options and focus on artworks that make a bold visual statement.

Explore by Artist or Art Movement: Delve deeper into specific artists or art movements that intrigue you by utilizing filters to narrow your search accordingly. Whether you're a fan of Renaissance masters or contemporary street artists, filtering your search by artist or art movement allows you to explore a curated selection of artworks that resonate with your artistic preferences. For example: imagine you're fascinated by the works of the Impressionist movement. By filtering your search to display artworks by renowned Impressionist artists such as Claude Monet or Edgar Degas, you can immerse yourself in the luminous landscapes and ethereal scenes that define this iconic artistic movement.

Set Price and Size Parameters: Define your budget and size preferences using filters to ensure that the artworks displayed align with your purchasing criteria. Whether you're seeking an investment piece or a statement artwork for your home, setting price and size parameters allows you to focus on artworks that fit within your budget and spatial constraints. For example: let's say you're in the market for a mid-sized sculpture to display in your office. By filtering your search to display sculptures priced between $500 and $1,000 and measuring under 24 inches in height, you can find the perfect piece that complements your space without breaking the bank.

Utilize Advanced Search Options: Take advantage of advanced search options offered by online art platforms to fine-tune your search based on specific criteria such as color palette, subject matter, or artistic technique. These advanced filters enable you to customize your search parameters and uncover artworks that resonate with your unique aesthetic preferences. For example: suppose you're looking for a serene landscape painting to add a sense of tranquility to your home. By utilizing advanced search options to filter artworks by color palette (e.g., calming blues and greens) and subject matter (e.g., landscapes), you can discover artworks that evoke a sense of serenity and harmony.

Save Favorites and Create Wishlists: As you browse through artworks, take advantage of features that allow you to save favorites and create wishlists for future reference. By bookmarking artworks that catch your eye, you can revisit them later, compare options, and ultimately make more informed purchasing decisions. For example: imagine you come across a striking contemporary sculpture that captures your imagination. By saving it to your favorites or adding it to a wishlist, you can keep track of the artwork and revisit it later to assess whether it's the right fit for your collection or space.

2 · **Explore Recommendations:** Take advantage of recommendation algorithms and personalized suggestions to discover artworks tailored to your interests and preferences. Many platforms use machine learning algorithms to analyze your browsing history and activity, providing recommendations based on your past interactions.

3 · **Engage with the Community:** Participate in online forums, discussions, and social media groups dedicated to art buying and collecting. Engaging with the art community can provide valuable insights, recommendations, and support from fellow enthusiasts and experts.

By incorporating these tips and strategies into your art browsing experience, you can streamline your search, uncover artworks that resonate with your preferences, and embark on a journey of discovery and exploration in the vibrant world of online art. Whether you're a seasoned collector or a novice enthusiast harnessing the power of filters and categories empowers you to curate a collection that reflects your unique tastes and passions. Use them as you please.

Understanding Auction Formats and Bidding Processes

Auctions are a cornerstone of the online art market, offering buyers the opportunity to acquire coveted artworks through competitive bidding. Understanding the different auction formats and bidding processes is essential for navigating these dynamic and fast-paced environments effectively. Here's an overview of the most common auction formats:

1 · **Live Auctions:** Live auctions take place in real-time, with bidders participating in the auction remotely via an online bidding platform. Bidders compete against each other by placing bids on artworks as the auctioneer conducts the sale, with the highest bidder winning the artwork at the conclusion of the auction.

2 · **Timed Auctions:** Timed auctions, also known as online-only auctions, allow bidders to place bids on artworks over a specified period, typically ranging from a few days to several weeks. Bidders submit their bids electronically, and the highest bid at the end of the auction wins the artwork.

3 · **Proxy Bidding:** Proxy bidding allows bidders to set a maximum bid amount on an artwork, with the auction platform automatically placing bids on their behalf up to their maximum bid. This allows bidders to participate in auctions without constantly monitoring the bidding activity.

By familiarizing yourself with the different auction formats and bidding processes, you'll be better equipped to navigate online auctions with confidence and strategy, maximizing your chances of acquiring the artworks you desire.

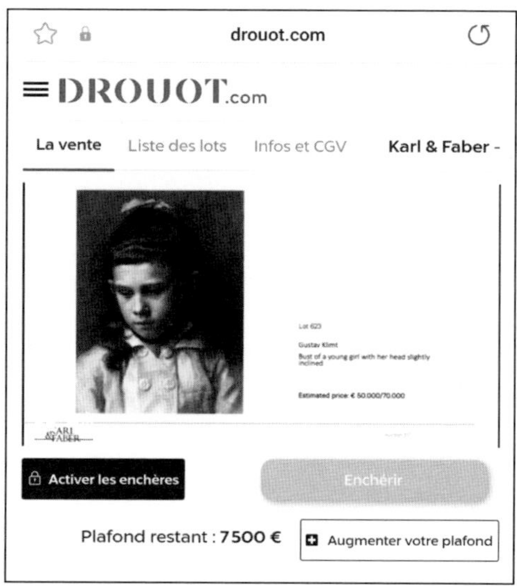

Harnessing the Power of Social Media: The Rise of Instagram in Online Art Buying

In today's digital age, social media platforms play a pivotal role in shaping the way we discover, consume, and interact with art. Among these platforms, Instagram stands out as a powerhouse for connecting artists, collectors, and enthusiasts from around the world. With its visual-centric approach and vast user base, Instagram has become an indispensable tool for navigating the online art market and discovering new talent.

Discovering Emerging Artists: One of the most significant benefits of Instagram for art buyers is its ability to showcase the work of emerging artists. Through hashtags, geotags, and curated feeds, users can explore a diverse range of artistic styles and perspectives, uncovering hidden gems and emerging talents that may not yet have gained mainstream recognition. For collectors seeking to add fresh, contemporary pieces to their collections, Instagram provides a direct line to the latest trends and up-and-coming artists.

Building Connections: Beyond mere discovery, Instagram facilitates meaningful connections between artists, collectors, and galleries. Through direct messaging, comments, and engagement with posts, users can forge relationships with artists and galleries, leading to collaborations, commissions, and even acquisitions. By fostering a sense of community and dialogue, Instagram transforms the art-buying experience into a dynamic and interactive process, where collectors can engage directly with the creators behind the works they admire.

Navigating the Market: In addition to connecting with individual artists, Instagram serves as a valuable resource for navigating the broader art market. Galleries, auction houses, and art institutions often maintain a presence on the platform, sharing updates on exhibitions, events, and available artworks. By following these accounts, collectors can stay informed about upcoming opportunities, track market trends, and gain insights into the latest developments in the art world.

Facilitating Transactions: Instagram's e-commerce features, such as shoppable posts and integrated checkout options, have further streamlined the art-buying process. Artists and galleries can showcase their works directly on their Instagram profiles, providing detailed descriptions, pricing information, and purchase options. For collectors, this means the ability to browse, inquire about, and even purchase artworks with just a few taps on their smartphone screen, transforming Instagram into a virtual marketplace for art enthusiasts.

Challenges and Considerations: While Instagram offers numerous opportunities for art buyers, it also presents challenges and considerations that should not be overlooked. As with any online platform, authenticity, provenance, and quality can be difficult to verify, requiring collectors to exercise caution and due diligence when making purchases. Additionally, the sheer volume of content on Instagram can be overwhelming, making it essential for collectors to curate their feeds and focus on accounts that align with their interests and preferences.

In conclusion, Instagram has emerged as a powerful tool for navigating the online art market, offering unparalleled opportunities for discovery, engagement, and transaction. By harnessing the platform's features and capabilities, collectors can connect with artists, galleries, and fellow enthusiasts in ways that were previously unimaginable, revolutionizing the art-buying experience in the digital age.

The Emerging Power of Artificial Intelligence in Online Art Buying

In the digital age, the integration of artificial intelligence (AI) technologies has revolutionized the way we approach online art buying, offering unprecedented opportunities for collectors to enhance their purchasing experiences and make more informed decisions. From personalized recommendations to advanced image recognition capabilities, AI is reshaping the landscape of the art market and empowering collectors with new tools and insights. In this section, we'll explore how AI is used and its utility in online art buying.

1 · Personalized Recommendations: AI-powered recommendation systems analyze user preferences, browsing history, and interaction patterns to generate personalized recommendations tailored to each individual collector's tastes and interests. By leveraging machine learning algorithms, online art platforms can curate a selection of artworks that are likely to resonate with each collector, facilitating more meaningful and relevant discovery experiences.

Example: Imagine you're browsing an online art platform and have previously shown an affinity for abstract paintings in vibrant colors. Through AI-powered recommendation algorithms, the platform suggests a curated selection of abstract artworks that align with your preferences, making it easier for you to discover new artists and styles that appeal to you.

2 · Image Recognition and Search: AI-based image recognition technology enables users to search for artworks using visual cues, such as colors, shapes, and compositions. By analyzing the visual features of artworks, AI algorithms can identify similar pieces based on their visual characteristics, allowing collectors to explore a diverse range of artworks that share common aesthetic traits.

Example: Suppose you come across a captivating artwork but are unsure how to describe it in words. Using AI-powered image recognition search, you can upload an image of the artwork and instantly find similar pieces that match its visual style, enabling you to explore related artworks and discover new favorites.

3 · Market Analysis and Trends Prediction: AI algorithms analyze vast amounts of data, including auction results, market trends, and artist performance metrics, to provide collectors with insights into the dynamics of the art market and predict future trends. By leveraging predictive analytics, collectors can make more informed decisions about buying and selling artworks, capitalizing on emerging opportunities and minimizing risks.

Example: AI-powered market analysis tools forecast a growing demand for contemporary sculpture by emerging artists based on an analysis of recent auction results and collector preferences. Armed with this insight, collectors may choose to invest in contemporary sculpture by up-and-coming artists, anticipating potential appreciation in value over time.

4 · Authentication and Fraud Detection: Some AI technologies are already employed to authenticate artworks and detect potential fraudulent practices, such as forgery, misattribution, and alteration. By analyzing various data points, including provenance records, technical details, and stylistic characteristics, AI algorithms can flag suspicious artworks and alert collectors to potential risks before making a purchase. These technologies are in constant development; make sure to find the most updated one.

Example: An AI-based authentication system could help you examine a high-value artwork attributed to a renowned artist and identifies inconsistencies in the brushwork and signature, raising doubts about its authenticity. This would alert the collector to conduct further investigation and seek expert opinion to verify the artwork's legitimacy.

5 · Enhanced User Experience: AI-driven chatbots and virtual assistants provide personalized support and guidance to users throughout the art buying process, offering real-time assistance, answering questions, and addressing concerns. By leveraging natural language processing and machine learning capabilities, these AI-powered assistants enhance the overall user experience and foster engagement with online art platforms.

Example: A collector browsing an online art platform interacts with an AI-powered chatbot to inquire about the availability of a specific artwork. The chatbot provides detailed information about the artwork, including its provenance, pricing, and shipping options, helping the collector make an informed decision and complete the purchase seamlessly.

In conclusion, the integration of artificial intelligence in online art buying offers a myriad of benefits for collectors, ranging from personalized recommendations and advanced search capabilities to market analysis and authentication services. As AI continues to evolve and innovate, its role in shaping the future of online art buying is poised to expand, unlocking new possibilities and opportunities for collectors around the world.

5

Assessing Authenticity and Condition

When buying art online, verifying the authenticity and condition of a piece is crucial. This chapter provides a practical guide to help you evaluate these aspects. We'll outline key factors to look for when determining if an artwork is genuine and in good condition, and offer tools and strategies to help you make well-informed purchasing decisions. With these insights, you'll be better prepared to navigate potential pitfalls and ensure a successful buying experience.

Identifying Red Flags for Authenticity

Ensuring the authenticity of an artwork is paramount when making a purchase, particularly in the online art market where the risk of encountering counterfeit or misrepresented pieces can be higher. Here are some red flags to watch out for when assessing the authenticity of artworks:

1 · **Lack of Provenance:** Provenance is the documented history of an artwork, detailing its ownership, exhibition history, and sales records. It acts as a chain of custody, establishing the artwork's legitimacy and historical context. An artwork with incomplete or unverifiable provenance can be a significant red flag. For instance, if a supposed Picasso painting lacks records of previous ownership or exhibitions, this gap in documentation should prompt further investigation. Reputable sellers should be able to provide a detailed provenance, and the absence of such information warrants caution. Additionally, fake or forged provenance documents can sometimes accompany counterfeit artworks, so scrutinize these records carefully.

2 · **Suspicious Signatures or Marks:** Signatures, monograms, and other identifying marks are critical for verifying an artwork's authenticity. Examine the artwork for signs of tampering or inconsistency in the signature. For example, a painting attributed to Claude Monet should have a signature that matches known examples of his handwriting style. Differences in the thickness of the brushstrokes, spelling variations, or unnatural placement can indicate a forgery. Furthermore, modern technology such as ultraviolet light and infrared reflectography can reveal hidden layers of paint or alterations that are not visible to the naked eye, providing additional insights into the authenticity of the signature.

3 · **Inconsistent Style or Execution:** An artist's style and technique are often unique and recognizable. Any significant deviation from an artist's known body of work can be cause for concern. For example, if a piece attributed to Jackson Pollock lacks the characteristic drip painting technique he is famous for or the overall composition and color scheme feel off, it might be a sign of inauthenticity. Deep dives into catalogues raisonnés, comprehensive, annotated

listings of all the known works of an artist, can provide benchmarks for comparison. Consulting art historians or specialists who are familiar with the artist's work can also provide expert validation.

4 · **Unusual Materials or Methods:** Pay close attention to the materials and techniques used. Anachronistic materials or methods can be a clear indicator of a forgery. For instance, if a purported Renaissance painting contains pigments or materials that were not available during the period, it's likely a modern creation. X-ray fluorescence (XRF) spectroscopy can be used to analyze the elemental composition of the materials, revealing whether they match the period and region the artwork is claimed to be from. Similarly, examining the canvas or paper type can offer clues; many artists favored specific materials, and deviations can be telling.

5 · **Forensic Analysis:** Forensic analysis of artworks involves various scientific methods to verify authenticity. Techniques such as radiocarbon dating can determine the age of organic materials like wood or canvas. This method can be particularly useful in identifying whether a piece is from the claimed period. Similarly, dendrochronology, the study of tree ring patterns, can date wooden panels used in paintings and sculptures.

6 · **Digital Authentication:** In the digital age, blockchain technology is becoming an innovative solution for maintaining the provenance and authenticity of artworks. Blockchain provides a decentralized, immutable ledger that tracks the history of an artwork, from creation to each sale, ensuring transparency and security. Art platforms are increasingly adopting this technology to combat fraud.

7 · **Consulting Experts:** When in doubt, consulting experts is invaluable. Art historians, conservators, and forensic experts can provide insights that go beyond what's visible to the naked eye. Additionally, reputable auction houses and galleries often have in-house specialists who can authenticate artworks.

Exactly one year ago, I encountered a striking painting attributed to a well-known Impressionist artist. The piece was captivating, but something felt off about the signature. Using a combination of ultraviolet light and consulting historical records, I discovered discrepancies that indicated the signature had been added later. Further investigation revealed the painting was a high-quality reproduction, not an original. This experience reinforced the importance of thorough research and leveraging technology in the authentication process.

By being vigilant and attentive to these red flags, you'll be better equipped to assess the authenticity of artworks and avoid potential pitfalls in the online art market.

Evaluating Condition Reports and Documentation

In addition to authenticity, evaluating the condition of an artwork is essential to ensuring its long-term value and enjoyment. Before making a purchase, be sure to review the condition report and documentation provided by the seller, which may include detailed descriptions, photographs, and assessments of the artwork's condition.

Pay close attention to any signs of damage, wear, or restoration, and consider how these factors may impact the artwork's overall value and aesthetic appeal. Look for clear and accurate descriptions of the artwork's condition, including any imperfections or flaws that may affect its appearance or structural integrity.

If possible, request additional photographs or information from the seller to supplement the condition report and ensure that you have a comprehensive understanding of the artwork's condition before making a decision. Remember, transparency and honesty are key when evaluating the condition of artworks; reputable sellers will be forthcoming with accurate and detailed information to help you make an informed choice.

It is within the buyer's rights to request more information. They should not hesitate to ask questions and request condition reports or additional images. It is clearly stated in the auction sales terms that the buyer had the opportunity to study the object and is purchasing with full knowledge. Therefore, it is very difficult to hold the auction house liable if upon receiving the item, there is a defect, damage, or an attribution issue. One can only hold the auction house accountable if there is a falsehood (e.g., the description states that the artwork is signed when it is not) or an intent to deceive (e.g., the images sent have been altered)—yes, it can happen.

Ethical and Legal conditions

Checking Interpol and Stolen Art Databases: As a preventive measure, potential buyers can check if the artwork they are interested in is listed on databases maintained by organizations such as Interpol for stolen artworks. These databases contain information about artworks reported as stolen or missing, allowing buyers to cross-reference the artwork's details with the database to ensure it is not flagged as stolen or subject to legal disputes.

Interpol has released a new application, free and available to everyone, to identify stolen objects. Searches can be made by artist name, but there is also an image recognition tool.

Vetting Sellers and Platforms: When purchasing art online, it is essential to vet sellers and platforms to ensure they adhere to legal and ethical standards. Buyers should research the reputation and credibility of sellers, including galleries, auction houses, and individual sellers to verify their legitimacy and track record. Additionally, buyers should review the terms and conditions of online platforms to understand their policies regarding authenticity, returns, and dispute resolution.

Avoiding Fraudulent Practices: Buyers should be wary of common fraudulent practices in the art market, such as misrepresentation, forgery, and false attribution. To mitigate the risk of falling victim to fraud, buyers should scrutinize artworks carefully, request additional documentation or provenance when necessary, and seek professional opinions from experts or appraisers. Additionally, buyers should be cautious of deals that seem too good to be true and exercise skepticism when encountering suspicious or unverified sellers.

Ensuring Secure Transactions and Buyer Protections

When purchasing art online, it's essential to prioritize security and protect yourself against potential risks and uncertainties. Here are some tips for ensuring secure transactions and buyer protections:

1 · Use Reputable Platforms: Stick to reputable online art platforms and auction houses with established track records and robust buyer protection policies. Look for platforms that offer secure payment methods, encrypted transactions, and guarantees of authenticity and condition.

2 · Read the Fine Print: Before making a purchase, carefully review the terms and conditions of sale, including the seller's return and refund policies, shipping and delivery terms, and any applicable fees or charges. Be sure to understand your rights and responsibilities as a buyer and clarify any questions or concerns with the seller before finalizing the transaction.

3 · Insist on Certificates of Authenticity: When purchasing high-value artworks, insist on obtaining a certificate of authenticity from the seller, which provides documented proof of the artwork's authenticity and provenance. A reputable seller should be able to provide verifiable documentation to support the authenticity of the artwork and offer assurances of its quality and value.

4 · Consider Insurance: Consider investing in insurance coverage for your art collection to protect against loss, damage, or theft. Many insurance providers offer specialized policies for art collectors that provide comprehensive coverage for artworks both at home and in transit.

By following these guidelines and taking proactive steps to ensure security and protection, you'll minimize risks and safeguard your investment in the online art market.

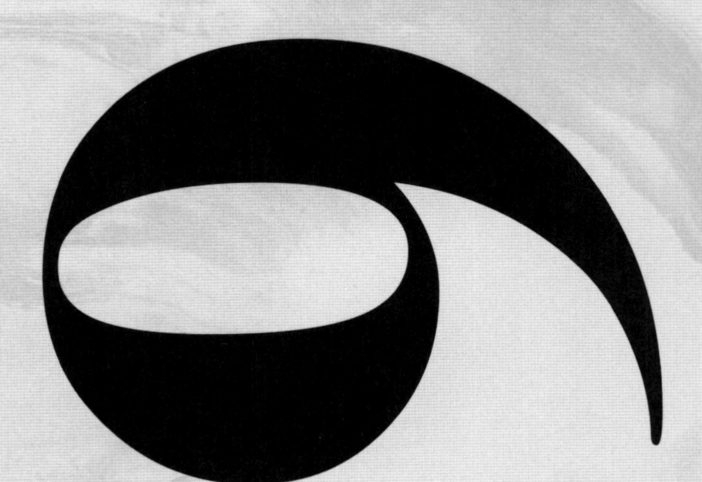

Tips for Successful Bidding

Ah, the exhilarating world of auctions—the thrill of the bid, the rush of competition, the sweet taste of victory. As you embark on your journey into the realm of online art buying, mastering the art of successful bidding is essential to securing the treasures that capture your imagination. In this chapter, we'll delve into the strategies, tactics, and mindset needed to navigate live and timed auctions with finesse and flair. So, sharpen your virtual paddle, dear reader, and let the bidding begin!

Strategies for Participating in Live Auctions

It is essential for art buyers to carefully assess their budget and consider all associated expenses before participating in an auction. The "hammer price" refers to the final bid amount accepted by the auctioneer, while the buyer's premium is an additional fee charged by the auction house. Shipping costs, restoration fees, and other potential expenses should also be factored in. By calculating these costs beforehand, buyers can establish a realistic limit on how much they are willing to spend, ensuring a smooth and transparent transaction process.

Live auctions are the epitome of excitement in the art-buying world, offering the thrill of bidding in real-time against fellow enthusiasts from around the globe. To emerge victorious in the fast-paced arena of live auctions, consider these strategies:

1 · **Know Your Limits:** The first and foremost rule of bidding is to know your financial boundaries. Begin by carefully assessing your budget, considering all associated costs. The hammer price refers to the final bid amount accepted by the auctioneer. However, this is not the total cost you'll incur. Auction houses typically charge a buyer's premium, which is an additional percentage of the hammer price. This premium can range from 15% to 25%, significantly affecting your final expenditure. Additionally, factor in shipping costs, especially if you're buying internationally. Artworks can be delicate and require specialized handling, which can add to the cost. Restoration fees might also be necessary if the piece requires any touch-ups or repairs. By calculating these expenses beforehand, you can establish a realistic limit on how much you are willing to spend, ensuring a smooth and transparent transaction process.

2 · **Stay Cool Under Pressure:** Live auctions are high-stakes environments where the adrenaline rush can cloud your judgment. It's easy to get swept up in the excitement and bid more than you initially intended. To avoid this, maintain a calm and focused demeanor. Have a firm maximum bid in mind and stick to it, regardless of how intense the bidding war becomes. Remember, there will always be other opportunities if you miss out on this one.

Bidding can be an exhilarating and adrenaline-fueled experience, but it's essential to maintain self-control and resist the urge to get caught up in the excitement of the moment. Take a deep breath, stay focused, and remind yourself of your financial limits and priorities before placing any bids.

Be Prepared to Walk Away: Sometimes, the best decision you can make in an auction is to walk away. If bidding exceeds your budget or if you feel uncomfortable with the pace or intensity of the auction, don't hesitate to bow out gracefully and regroup for the next opportunity. Remember, there will always be other artworks to bid on, but your financial well-being is priceless.

3 · **Timing is Everything:** Pay close attention to the pace of the auction and the rhythm of the bidding. Look for strategic opportunities to enter the fray when bidding slows down or hesitates, and be prepared to strike decisively when the moment is right.

4 · **Anticipate the Competition:** Study your fellow bidders and gauge their intentions and bidding patterns. Look for signs of hesitation or uncertainty, and be prepared to capitalize on opportunities to outmaneuver your competitors and secure the winning bid.

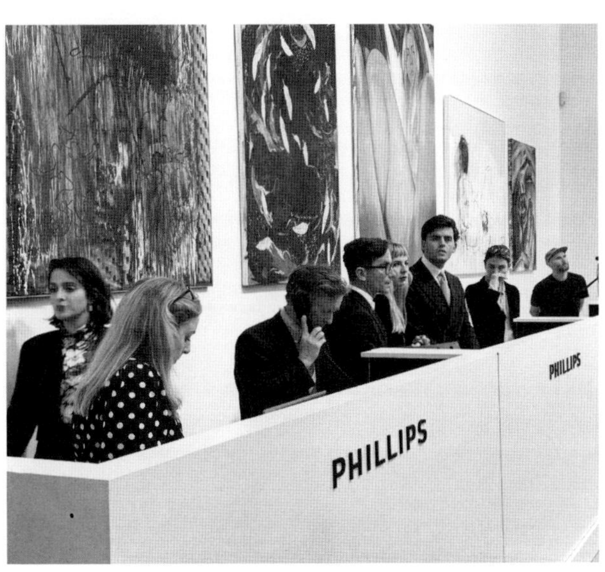

Maximizing Your Chances in Timed Auctions

Timed auctions offer a more relaxed and flexible bidding experience, allowing buyers to participate at their own pace over a specified period. To make the most of your time in a timed auction, consider these strategies:

1 · **Strategize Your Timing:** Avoid the temptation to place your bids too early in a timed auction, as this can drive up prices prematurely and diminish your chances of winning. Instead, wait until the closing minutes or seconds of the auction to make your move, strategically swooping in at the last moment to outbid your competitors.

2 · **Set Your Maximum Bid:** Determine your maximum bid amount in advance and enter it early in the auction to signal your intent and establish your presence. Be sure to set a bid that reflects the true value of the artwork to you, taking into account factors such as its condition, provenance, and rarity.

3 · **Stay Vigilant:** Keep a close eye on the progress of the auction and be prepared to adjust your bidding strategy as needed. Monitor competing bids, track the remaining time, and be ready to react swiftly to any last-minute challengers who may emerge.

4 · **Be Patient and Persistent:** Timed auctions can be a test of patience and persistence, requiring a steady hand and a keen eye for opportunity. Don't be discouraged by early setbacks or competing bids: stay focused, stay determined, and stay in the game until the very end.

5 · **Ensure a Stable Internet Connection:** A stable internet connection is crucial for participating in online auctions. A lag or disruption can cause you to miss out on critical moments. Make sure you have a reliable connection and consider using a wired connection for added stability.

6 · **Familiarize Yourself with the Platform:** Different auction platforms have varying interfaces and bidding processes. Spend some time exploring the platform before the auction begins. Understand

how to place a bid, set maximum bids, and follow the auction in real-time. Some platforms offer automated bidding features, where you can set your maximum bid, and the system will bid on your behalf up to that limit.

7 · Utilize Proxy Bidding: Many online auction platforms offer proxy bidding, allowing you to set a maximum bid in advance. The system will automatically place bids on your behalf, up to your specified limit. This can be especially useful if you cannot be online during the auction or if you want to avoid getting caught up in the excitement.

8 · Engage with Auctioneers and Specialists: Don't hesitate to reach out to the auction house's specialists or the auctioneer with any questions. They can provide additional information about the artwork, its provenance, and its condition. Building a rapport with these experts can also provide valuable insights and might give you an edge in understanding the artwork's true value.

Personal Insights:
Allow me to share a personal anecdote to highlight the importance of these strategies. During an online auction, I once found myself deeply interested in a mid-century abstract painting. I had set a clear budget, but the excitement of the bidding war tempted me to exceed it. However, remembering the importance of staying cool under pressure, I refrained. As the auction progressed, I noticed a competitor consistently placing bids just above mine. I strategically paused my bidding, waiting for the right moment when the pace slowed. This hesitation caused my competitor to lose momentum, and I placed a decisive final bid within my budget, securing the piece.

This experience reinforced the importance of patience, observation, and sticking to a well-planned strategy. It also underscored the joy and satisfaction that come from winning a bid through careful planning and execution, rather than impulse.

Successful bidding in live and online auctions requires a blend of strategy, discipline, and keen observation. By knowing your limits, staying calm under pressure, timing your bids strategically, and understanding your competition, you can navigate the auction world with confidence. Embrace the thrill of the chase, but always keep your financial goals and personal enjoyment in balance. Happy bidding!

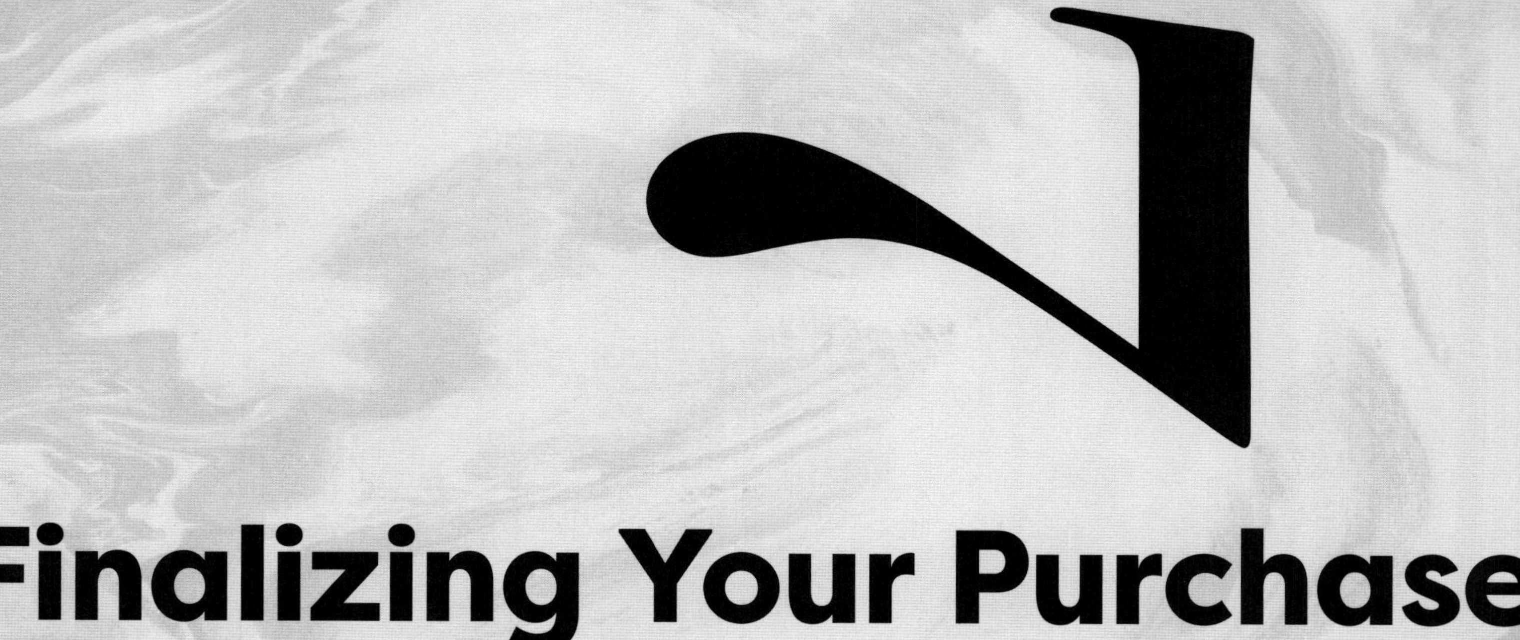

7 Finalizing Your Purchase

Congratulations! You've successfully navigated the exhilarating world of online art auctions and secured the perfect piece to add to your collection. Now, it's time to cross the finish line and finalize your purchase with confidence. In this chapter, we'll guide you through the essential steps of completing the purchase process, arranging shipping and delivery, and handling insurance and documentation, ensuring a smooth and seamless transaction from start to finish.

Cross the finish line with confidence!

Completing the Purchase Process

The devil is in the details.—German Proverb

With the bidding war behind you and the gavel fallen in your favor, it's time to seal the deal and officially make the artwork yours. Here's a step-by-step guide to completing the purchase process:

1 · **Confirming Your Bid:** Once the auction has ended, you'll receive confirmation (the Bordereau) of your winning bid via email or notification from the auction platform. Review the details of your bid carefully to ensure accuracy and confirm your intention to proceed with the purchase.

2 · **Payment:** Next, you'll need to arrange payment for the artwork according to the seller's specified payment methods and terms. Most online art platforms offer secure payment options, such as credit card, PayPal, bank or wire transfer, to facilitate a smooth and secure transaction. I've personally never had any sort of problems of this kind.

3 · **Reviewing Terms and Conditions:** Before finalizing your purchase, take the time to review the seller's terms and conditions of sale, including any applicable fees, taxes, or shipping costs. Be sure to understand your rights and responsibilities as a buyer and clarify any questions or concerns with the seller before proceeding.

4 · **Signing Contracts or Agreements:** In some cases, the seller may require you to sign contracts or agreements outlining the terms of the sale, including payment schedules, delivery arrangements, and any additional terms or conditions. Review these documents carefully and seek legal advice if necessary to ensure that you fully understand and agree to the terms. Take your time to do things properly. *Better to be safe than sorry.*—American Proverb

By completing these steps with diligence and attention to detail, you'll finalize your purchase with confidence and peace of mind, knowing that you've taken the necessary precautions to protect your investment and ensure a successful transaction.

Arranging Shipping and Delivery

Disclaimer: It's important to note that this book does not cover the intricacies of lots-shipping outside the European Union (EU) due to the complexity of international shipping regulations and customs procedures. While the principles and tips outlined in this guide are applicable to art buying within the EU, shipping items to destinations outside the EU may require additional research, expertise, and logistical considerations beyond the scope of this book. Readers interested in shipping lots internationally are encouraged to seek professional guidance and consult with shipping providers familiar with the specific requirements and regulations of their destination countries.

So, with the purchase process complete, it's time to turn your attention to arranging shipping and delivery for your newly acquired artwork. Here's what you need to know:

1 · **Communicating with the Seller:** Reach out to the seller promptly to discuss shipping and delivery arrangements for the artwork. Provide any necessary shipping information, such as your preferred shipping address and contact details, and confirm the estimated timeline for delivery.

2 · **Choosing a Shipping Method:** Consider your options for shipping and choose a method that best suits your needs and preferences. Factors to consider include the size and fragility of the artwork, the shipping destination, and any special handling requirements.

Select the right one: When it comes to shipping valuable artworks, not all shipping providers are created equal. It's essential to choose a reputable and experienced shipping company with a proven track record of handling fine art and antiques. Look for providers that offer specialized art shipping services, including custom crating, climate-controlled storage, and white-glove delivery.

Custom Crating and Packaging: Proper packaging is paramount to safeguarding your artwork during transit. Opt for custom crating and packaging services that are specifically designed to protect delicate and valuable artworks from damage caused by bumps, vibrations, and fluctuations in temperature and humidity.

Insurance Coverage: Despite your best efforts to ensure a smooth shipping process, accidents can still happen. Protect your investment by obtaining comprehensive insurance coverage for your artwork during transit. Verify that your chosen shipping provider offers adequate insurance options to provide financial protection in the event of loss, damage, or theft.

White-Glove Delivery Services: For larger or more delicate artworks, consider opting for white-glove delivery services that provide professional installation and setup in your home or gallery. These services typically include handling, unpacking, placement, and even wall mounting, ensuring that your artwork is displayed to perfection upon arrival.

By partnering with reputable shipping providers, investing in custom packaging, securing adequate insurance coverage, and opting for white-glove delivery services, you can rest assured that your artwork will reach its destination safely and securely. With the right preparations in place, you can enjoy peace of mind knowing that your precious investment is in good hands throughout its journey.

3 · Tracking Your Shipment: Once your artwork has been shipped, monitor its progress closely using the tracking information provided by the shipping carrier. Stay in communication with the seller and shipping carrier to ensure a smooth and timely delivery process.

By taking proactive steps to arrange shipping and delivery, you'll ensure that your artwork arrives safely and securely at its destination, ready to be enjoyed and admired for years to come.

Finally, going to collect a lot oneself is also a great opportunity to travel. If the lot is not too large and easily transportable, why not take a train and organize a little trip? Let's go!

Handling Insurance and Documentation

As a responsible art collector, it's essential to protect your investment by securing adequate insurance coverage for your artwork. Here's what you need to know about handling insurance and documentation:

1 · Obtaining Insurance Coverage: Contact your insurance provider to inquire about specialized insurance coverage for your art collection. Many insurance companies offer policies tailored to the unique needs of art collectors, providing comprehensive coverage for loss, damage, or theft of your artworks both at home and in transit.

2 · Documenting Your Art Collection: Keep detailed records of your art collection, including purchase receipts, certificates of authenticity, appraisals, and condition reports. These documents provide valuable documentation of the provenance, authenticity, and value of your artworks and can be essential for insurance purposes, estate planning, and resale.

3 · Reviewing Insurance Policies: Review your insurance policies regularly to ensure that your coverage adequately reflects the value and scope of your art collection. Update your policy as needed to account for any changes or additions to your collection and to maintain adequate coverage levels.

4 · Understanding Policy Limitations: Be aware of any limitations or exclusions in your insurance policy, such as coverage limits, deductibles, and exclusions for certain types of loss or damage. Work with your insurance provider to address any gaps in coverage and explore options for additional protection as needed.

By proactively managing your insurance coverage and documentation, you'll safeguard your art collection against potential risks and uncertainties, ensuring that your investment remains protected and secure for generations to come.

8

Building and Managing Your Collection

Becoming an art collector, whether you started online or in the "real" world, is more than simply acquiring artworks—it's about curating and caring for your collection with intention and dedication. In this chapter, we'll explore what it means to truly manage and nurture your collection. From preserving and displaying your artworks to strategically expanding your collection, you'll learn how to make decisions that reflect both your personal tastes and the value of each piece.

We'll cover essential topics like how to protect and maintain your artworks to ensure their longevity, as well as how to track market trends that may influence your future acquisitions. Most importantly, we'll discuss how to build your collection with purpose, allowing your passion for art to shine through every new addition.

Don't hesitate to continue evolving and expanding your collection, and remember that each piece adds to the artistic legacy you're building.

Displaying and Preserving Your Artworks

Now that you've acquired your prized artworks, it's time to give them the attention they deserve by displaying them in your home or workspace. Here are some tips for displaying and preserving your artworks:

1 · **Choose the Right Location:** Select a suitable location in your home or office to display your artworks, taking into account factors such as lighting, space, and visibility. Avoid placing artworks in direct sunlight or areas prone to temperature fluctuations or humidity, as these conditions can damage the artworks over time.

2 · **Frame and Mount Artworks:** Invest in high-quality frames and mounts to protect and enhance the presentation of your artworks. Choose frames that complement the style and aesthetic of the artwork while providing adequate support and protection against damage.

3 · **Rotate Artworks Regularly:** Keep your collection fresh and dynamic by rotating artworks regularly and experimenting with different display configurations. This not only allows you to enjoy your entire collection but also helps to prevent damage from prolonged exposure to light and environmental factors.

4 · **Invest in Conservation:** Consider investing in professional conservation services to preserve and maintain the condition of your artworks over time. Conservation treatments such as cleaning, repair, and restoration can help to address any damage or deterioration and ensure that your artworks remain in pristine condition for generations to come.

Tracking Your Collection and Market Trends

As your collection grows and evolves, it's essential to stay informed about market trends and developments in the art world. Here are some strategies for tracking your collection and market trends:

1 · Maintain Detailed Records: Keep detailed records of your art collection, including purchase receipts, certificates of authenticity, appraisals, and condition reports. Use a dedicated database or inventory management system to track important information about each artwork, including its provenance, acquisition history, and current value.

2 · Research Market Trends: Stay informed about market trends and developments by reading art publications, attending exhibitions and art fairs, and networking with fellow collectors and industry professionals. Pay attention to emerging artists, new movements, and shifting tastes and preferences in the art market.

3 · Monitor Auction Results: Keep an eye on auction results and sales data to track the performance of artworks by artists in your collection and to identify emerging trends and market opportunities. Online auction databases and market analysis reports can provide valuable insights into pricing trends, demand levels, and market dynamics.

There are paid platforms that allow you to consult price data and analyze artists' profiles, such as Artprice or Artnet. They are not expensive and they are a worthwhile investment and a useful tool if you want to collect art seriously.

4 · Consult with Experts: Seek advice and guidance from art advisors, curators, and other industry experts to help inform your collecting decisions and navigate the complexities of the art market. Build relationships with trusted professionals who can provide expert opinions, appraisals, and assistance with acquisitions and sales.

Tips for Expanding and Diversifying Your Collection

As a collector, it's essential to continually expand and diversify your collection to keep it dynamic and vibrant. Here are some tips for expanding and diversifying your collection:

1 · Explore New Artists and Genres: Diving into the art world is like embarking on a grand adventure, full of unknown territories and hidden treasures. One of the most exhilarating parts of this journey is exploring new artists and genres. While it's easy to fall into the comfort of familiar styles and well-known names, pushing your boundaries can lead to discovering truly remarkable pieces that resonate on a deeper level.

Embracing the Unknown: To begin this exploration, start by immersing yourself in various art forms that you might not typically gravitate towards. Visit local galleries and museums, not just the big names but also the small, independent ones that often showcase up-and-coming talent. Attend diverse exhibitions that feature a range of styles—from contemporary and abstract to street art and digital installations. Online platforms have revolutionized how we discover art. Websites like Artsy, Saatchi Art, and Behance offer vast collections of artworks by emerging and established artists from around the globe. Social media, particularly Instagram, is an invaluable tool for art discovery. Follow a mix of artists, galleries, and art fairs to keep your feed vibrant and diverse. Engage with posts, join live sessions, and don't hesitate to slide into an artist's DMs to ask about their work. Many artists appreciate direct engagement and are happy to share insights about their creative process.

Breaking Out of Comfort Zones: To truly expand your horizons, make it a point to explore genres that are completely outside your usual preferences. If you primarily collect modernist paintings, consider exploring the world of kinetic art, which involves moving parts and viewer interaction. Or delve into the realm of digital art and NFTs, which have been making waves in the art market and offer a unique blend of technology and creativity.

The Joy of Discovery: The joy of discovering new artists lies in the stories behind their creations. Each piece is a window into the artist's world, reflecting their experiences, struggles, and triumphs. When you explore new artists, you're not just adding an artwork to your collection, you're inviting a part of their journey into your life.

Engage with these artists; attend their talks, read their interviews, and follow their careers. This not only enhances your appreciation of their work but also builds a personal connection that enriches your collecting experience. For instance, discovering a young, struggling artist and watching them grow into a celebrated figure can be incredibly rewarding. You become a part of their narrative and their success feels like a shared victory.

2 · Set Acquisition Goals: While spontaneity has its charm, setting specific acquisition goals can transform your collecting journey into a purposeful and enriching endeavor. By establishing clear objectives, you create a framework that guides your decisions and ensures that your collection evolves in a coherent and meaningful way.

Defining Your Vision: Start by reflecting on what you want your collection to represent. Are you interested in a particular historical period, cultural movement, or artistic style? Perhaps you want to focus on contemporary artists who challenge societal norms or explore themes of environmental sustainability. Your goals should align with your personal interests and values, making your collection a true reflection of your passions.

For instance, I once decided to focus a part of my collection on artworks that explore the theme of migration. This decision stemmed from my personal interest in stories of human movement and cultural exchange. I sought out artists whose works delved into these narratives, attending exhibitions and talks that explored these themes. This focus not only enriched my collection but also deepened my understanding of a subject close to my heart.

Creating a Roadmap: Once you have a clear vision, break it down into actionable steps. Set short-term and long-term goals that guide your acquisitions. Short-term goals might include attending a certain number of exhibitions per year or acquiring works from a specific list of emerging artists. Long-term goals could involve building a comprehensive collection that covers an entire artistic movement or historical period.

For example, if your long-term goal is to create a collection of post-war abstract expressionist works, your short-term goals might include acquiring key pieces from lesser-known artists of the movement, attending relevant auctions, and networking with experts in the field. This structured approach ensures that each acquisition contributes to the overarching narrative of your collection.

Balancing Diversity and Cohesion: While it's important to diversify your collection, maintaining a sense of cohesion is equally crucial.

Your acquisition goals should help you strike this balance. Diversity can be achieved through various means—geographical, cultural, temporal, or stylistic differences. However, there should be a unifying thread that ties your collection together.

For instance, you might focus on contemporary art but include works from artists across different continents. The unifying element could be the exploration of contemporary societal issues, with each piece offering a unique cultural perspective. This approach not only diversifies your collection but also creates a rich tapestry of interconnected narratives.

Leveraging Technology and Expertise: In the digital age, setting acquisition goals can be greatly enhanced by leveraging technology and expert advice. Utilize art market databases like Artprice and Artnet to track trends and gather data on artists and their works. These platforms provide valuable insights into pricing, historical sales data, and artist rankings, helping you make informed decisions.

Additionally, consider consulting with art advisors or curators who specialize in your area of interest. Their expertise can provide nuanced perspectives and guide your acquisitions in line with your goals. Building relationships with gallery owners and auction house specialists can also open doors to exclusive opportunities and insider knowledge.

3 · Attend Art Fairs and Events: Art fairs, festivals, and cultural events are bustling hubs of creativity and innovation. They offer a unique opportunity to immerse yourself in the vibrant world of contemporary art and discover new artists and galleries. Events like Art Basel, Frieze, and the Venice Biennale showcase a wide range of artworks from emerging and established artists. Use these occasions to meet artists, gallerists, and fellow collectors, expanding your network within the art community. Engaging in conversations and attending panel discussions at these events can also provide valuable insights into current trends and the evolving art market.

4 · Support Emerging Artists: Consider supporting emerging artists by acquiring their artworks early in their careers and following their development over time. Investing in emerging talent not only provides financial support to artists but also allows you to participate in the excitement of discovering and nurturing new voices in the art world. Platforms like Instagram, Kickstarter, and various online galleries are excellent for discovering up-and-coming artists. Additionally, university art shows and local artist collectives can be treasure troves of fresh talent. By fostering relationships with these artists, you contribute to their growth and can witness firsthand how their art evolves.

Deepening Your Collection

To build a truly comprehensive collection, delve deeper into the technical and historical aspects of the artworks you acquire:

1 · **Provenance and Documentation:** Ensure that each piece in your collection has a well-documented provenance. This includes previous ownership, exhibition history, and any literature references. Provenance not only adds value but also authenticity to your collection. In cases of older or historical works, thorough documentation can prevent legal issues and establish a clear lineage.

2 · **Condition and Restoration:** Regularly assess the condition of your artworks and consider professional restoration if needed. Works on paper, for example, can be prone to discoloration and brittleness over time. Paintings may require cleaning or touch-ups to maintain their original vibrancy. Investing in proper restoration and conservation ensures the longevity of your collection.

3 · **Thematic and Curatorial Approaches:** Consider adopting a thematic or curatorial approach to your collection. This could involve focusing on specific themes such as social justice, environmental issues, or technological advancements. A thematic collection can create a cohesive narrative and provide deeper insightsinto the chosen subject matter. For instance, a collection centered around climate change might include works from various mediums and perspectives, sparking critical conversations and reflections.

Personal Insights and Anecdotes

A few years ago, I attended an art fair in Berlin, primarily to explore contemporary European art. However, I stumbled upon a booth showcasing traditional African sculptures. The intricate craftsmanship and cultural significance of the pieces captivated me. Despite initially having no intention of purchasing traditional art, I decided to acquire a stunning mask that symbolized ancestral reverence. This purchase not only enriched my collection but also opened my eyes to the profound connections between different art forms and cultural expressions.

Fine Art Consultants: Guiding Your Art Journey

As you navigate the intricate and exhilarating world of art collecting, you might find yourself in need of expert guidance. This is where Fine Art Consultants come into play. These professionals serve as invaluable resources, offering expertise and insights that can enhance your collecting experience and help you make informed decisions. Whether you're buying art online or offline, the role of a Fine Art Consultant is crucial in the context of this book.

The Role of a Fine Art Consultant

Fine art consultants are professionals who provide specialized advice and services to art collectors, institutions, and corporations. Their expertise spans various aspects of the art world, including art history, market trends, valuation, and conservation. Here's a deeper look into their roles and how they can benefit you as a collector:

1 · **Expert Guidance and Education:** Fine art consultants possess extensive knowledge of art history, styles, and movements. They can educate you about different artists, periods, and genres, helping you refine your tastes and preferences. Whether you're a novice or an experienced collector, their insights can deepen your understanding and appreciation of art.

2 · **Art Acquisition and Curation:** Consultants can assist you in identifying and acquiring artworks that align with your goals and tastes. They have access to a vast network of galleries, auction houses, and private dealers, providing you with opportunities to acquire

rare and significant pieces. Additionally, they can help curate your collection, ensuring it remains cohesive and reflects your vision.

3 · **Valuation and Investment Advice:** Understanding the value of art is essential for making informed purchasing decisions. Fine art consultants can provide accurate valuations based on current market trends and historical data. If you view art as an investment, they can offer advice on potential future appreciation and the best times to buy or sell.

4 · **Provenance and Authenticity:** One of the most critical aspects of collecting art is ensuring the authenticity and provenance of the pieces. Consultants conduct thorough research and due diligence to verify the history and legitimacy of artworks. This expertise is particularly valuable in the online art market, where the risk of encountering forgeries is higher.

5 · **Negotiation and Transaction Management:** Buying art often involves complex negotiations and legal considerations. Fine art consultants can handle these aspects on your behalf, ensuring that transactions are smooth and transparent. They can negotiate prices, review contracts, and manage logistics, allowing you to focus on the joy of collecting.

Fine Art Consultants in the Online Art World

The digital age has transformed the way we buy and sell art, and fine art consultants have adapted to this shift. In the online art market, their role is more critical than ever:

1 · **Navigating Online Platforms:** With numerous online galleries and auction platforms, finding the right artwork can be overwhelming. Consultants can guide you through these platforms, helping you identify reputable sellers and worthwhile pieces. They stay updated on the latest digital trends and technologies, ensuring you make informed decisions in the online space.

2 · **Virtual Consultations:** Many consultants offer virtual consultations, allowing you to benefit from their expertise regardless of your location. Through video calls and online presentations,

they can provide personalized advice and recommendations, making the art world more accessible than ever.

3 · Digital Tools and Analytics: Fine art consultants leverage digital tools and analytics to provide data-driven insights. They use market analysis software, provenance databases, and digital catalogues to research and verify artworks. These tools enhance their ability to provide accurate valuations and identify investment opportunities.

The Personal Touch

Working with a fine art consultant adds a personal touch to your collecting journey. Their role goes beyond technical expertise; they become your confidant and partner in the art world. Here's a personal anecdote to illustrate this point:

A few years ago, I was interested in acquiring a piece by a contemporary artist whose work I admired. I sought the advice of a fine art consultant, a good friend of mine, who not only provided detailed insights into the artist's career and market value but also shared personal stories and encounters with the artist. This enriched my understanding and appreciation of the artwork. The consultant also managed the entire acquisition process, from negotiating the price to arranging for secure shipping. Their involvement transformed what could have been a simple transaction into a meaningful and memorable experience.

Fine art consultants play an important role in the art collecting journey, offering expertise that spans the art market's intricacies. Whether you're buying art online or offline, their guidance can help you make informed decisions, ensuring that your collection is both valuable and meaningful. By leveraging their knowledge and networks, you can navigate the art world with confidence, knowing that you have a trusted advisor by your side. Embrace the collaboration with a fine art consultant as an integral part of your collecting strategy, enriching your journey with wisdom, expertise, and personal connection.

Expanding and diversifying your art collection is a continuous journey of exploration and learning. By exploring new artists and genres, setting specific acquisition goals, attending art fairs and events, and supporting emerging artists, you can cultivate a rich and diverse artistic legacy. Remember, collecting art is not just about acquiring objects; it's about fostering connections, exploring ideas, and enriching your life with beauty and meaning. Make collecting an endless process, an attitude that reflects your passion, curiosity, and commitment to the arts. Embrace the journey with enthusiasm, and let your collection be a testament to your evolving tastes and the stories you wish to tell.

The Pivotal Role of Art Marchands and Gallerists

Despite the digital revolution, the role of the art marchand and gallerists remains crucial and far from obsolete. These professionals continue to play a vital role in the art ecosystem by curating selections, providing provenance, and offering expert guidance to collectors. They foster relationships with artists and buyers, ensuring that the human element of art appreciation and acquisition is maintained. Their expertise and eye for quality cannot be replicated by algorithms or online platforms.

Art marchands and gallerists have a deep understanding of the art market and its trends. They can identify emerging artists and promote their work to the right audience. Their curated exhibitions and sales provide a context for the art, helping collectors understand its significance and value. This curation is essential for maintaining the integrity of the art market, ensuring that quality and originality are prioritized over trends and hype.

Moreover, art marchands and gallerists provide essential services that go beyond the sale. They offer provenance research, ensuring the authenticity and history of an artwork. This is particularly important in a market where forgeries and misattributions can be a significant risk. They also provide conservation advice, helping collectors preserve their artworks for future generations.

While the digital art world has opened doors, it's the seasoned eye and discerning taste of a skilled marchand or gallerist that often make the difference between a good collection and a great one. Let's not kid ourselves: knowing what to buy and what to avoid is an art form in itself.

Building Relationships: One of the most important roles of art marchands and gallerists is building relationships. They act as intermediaries between artists and collectors, facilitating connections that are beneficial to both parties. These relationships are built on trust and mutual respect, and they often result in long-term collaborations.

For artists, having a gallerist or marchand can be crucial for their career development. These professionals provide not only financial support through sales but also mentorship and guidance. They help artists navigate the complexities of the art market, from pricing their work to understanding legal and contractual issues. This support allows artists to focus on their creative practice, knowing that their career is in capable hands.

Gallerists often serve as career shepherds for artists, guiding them through the labyrinthine art world. Take Jean, a young sculptor who struggled to find her footing until she partnered with a well-regarded gallery. "They helped me find my voice and market my work effectively," she says. "Without their support, I'd still be toiling in obscurity."

For collectors, the relationship with a gallerist or marchand is equally important. These professionals provide personalized advice and recommendations, helping collectors build cohesive and valuable collections. They offer insights into market trends and investment potential, ensuring that collectors make informed decisions. This guidance is particularly valuable for new collectors, who may be unfamiliar with the nuances of the art market.

Consider David, a novice collector who stumbled into his first gallery with more curiosity than knowledge. "I knew I loved art, but I didn't know where to start," he recalls. "The gallerist didn't just sell me pieces—they educated me, helped me refine my taste, and introduced me to artists whose work resonated deeply with me."

Creating Cultural Experiences: Art marchands and gallerists also create meaningful cultural experiences through exhibitions and events that build community and offer deeper engagement with art. Their physical spaces serve as hubs for dialogue and discovery, bridging the gap between the digital and physical art worlds. These events provide opportunities for collectors to meet artists, engage with their work, and participate in discussions about contemporary art.

Exhibitions curated by gallerists often have a thematic or conceptual focus, providing context and depth to the artworks on display. This curatorial approach enhances the viewer's understanding and appreciation of the art. It also creates a narrative that connects individual works, making the exhibition more than just a collection of objects.

Gallerists and marchands also organize artist talks, panel discussions, and workshops, providing educational opportunities for collectors and the general public. These events foster a sense of community and encourage a deeper engagement with art. They also provide a platform for artists to share their ideas and process, enriching the viewer's experience.

Rebecca, a frequent gallery-goer, treasures these experiences. "It's not just about buying art; it's about being part of a conversation," she explains. "I've learned so much from gallerists who take the time to explain an artist's vision or the significance of a particular piece. Those insights are priceless."

The Backbone of Stability: In a rapidly evolving art market, art marchands and gallerists provide the backbone of stability. They bring historical perspective, having seen market trends come and go. Their deep expertise helps to prevent the art market from becoming another speculative bubble akin to the cryptocurrency or finance booms that ended in busts.

The traditional art market has always been susceptible to trends and speculations, but the knowledgeable guidance of gallerists ensures that buyers invest in works of lasting value. They understand the importance of authenticity and provenance, elements that cannot be compromised if the market is to maintain its credibility. Their role in educating and advising collectors safeguards against impulsive purchases driven by hype.

Art marchands and gallerists also play a critical role in the vetting process. In an era where digital art and NFTs can be created and sold with relative ease, the risk of fraud and forgery is ever-present. Experienced gallerists ensure that only genuine, high-quality works reach collectors. This vetting process is essential for maintaining trust in the market and ensuring that investments in art are secure.

Looking to the Future: As the art world continues to navigate the digital revolution, the role of art marchands and gallerists will remain indispensable. They will continue to adapt, leveraging technology to enhance their services while maintaining the personal touch that defines their profession. Their expertise will be crucial in guiding collectors through the complexities of both the physical and digital art markets.

In the future, we can expect to see a hybrid model where online and offline experiences complement each other. Virtual exhibitions will provide global reach, while physical galleries will offer the tactile and emotional engagement that only in-person viewing can provide. Gallerists and marchands will be at the forefront of this evolution, ensuring that the art market remains vibrant, credible, and deeply connected to its historical roots.

So, next time you find yourself lost in the digital expanse of an online art marketplace or captivated by a virtual exhibition, remember the gallerists and marchands behind the scenes. They're not just selling art: they're preserving its soul, ensuring that even in a world driven by clicks, the profound human connection to art remains as vibrant and essential as ever. They are the guardians against the potential pitfalls of a speculative bubble, providing the expertise and stability needed to sustain the art market's future.

In a world where technology changes at lightning speed, the wisdom and guidance of seasoned art professionals are more valuable than ever. They ensure that the art market evolves without losing its essence, balancing innovation with tradition, and making sure that the art we collect today continues to inspire and resonate for generations to come.

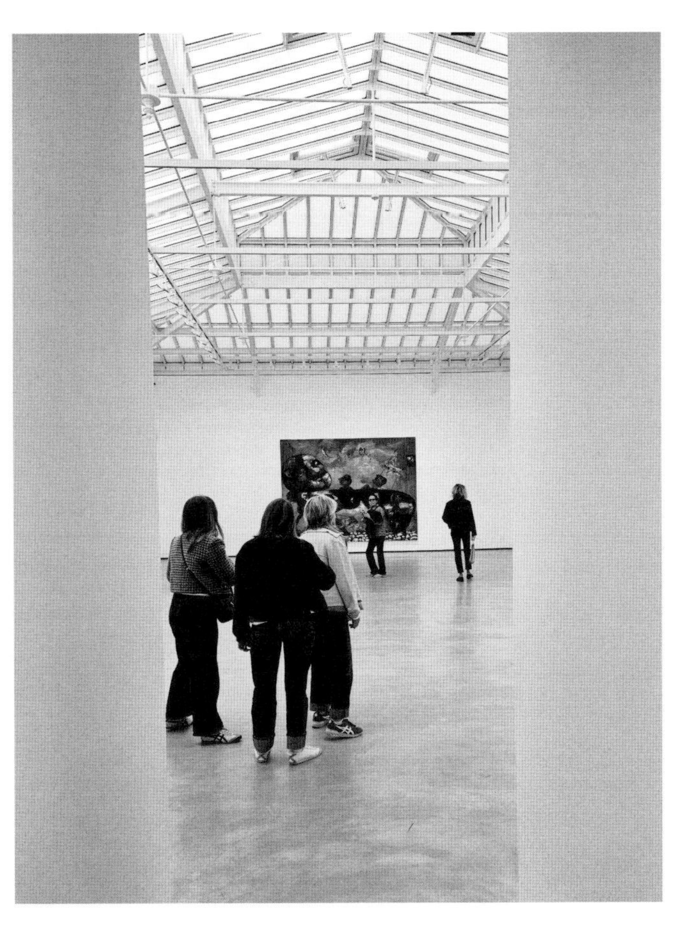

9

End of This Journey

As you stand at the threshold of the concluding chapter of your online art buying journey, take a moment to bask in the glow of your accomplishments. You've navigated the treacherous waters of the digital art market with the grace of a seasoned sailor, braving storms of uncertainty and riding waves of excitement to reach the shores of success. Now, as you prepare to bid adieu to this guide, let's embark on one final voyage of reflection and celebration.

Reflecting on Your Online Art Buying Journey

Cast your mind back to the beginning of your odyssey: the eager anticipation, the trembling excitement, the nagging doubts that whispered in the recesses of your mind. Remember the thrill of your first bid, the rush of adrenaline as the auction timer counted down, and the victorious jubilation as the gavel fell in your favor. You've traversed virtual galleries, scaled digital auction houses, and uncovered hidden treasures that spark joy and inspiration in your soul.

But beyond the acquisitions, the mistakes and victories lies a deeper journey—a journey of self-discovery, exploration, and growth. You've honed your eye for beauty, refined your taste for excellence, and forged connections with artists, collectors, and enthusiasts from every corner of the globe. You've learned to trust your instincts, embrace your passions, and chart your own course through the vast and turbulent seas of the art world.

Mistakes? Yes indeed.

Making mistakes is an inherent part of the art-collecting journey, but it's important to recognize that these missteps can lead to valuable lessons and unexpected outcomes. Whether it's overpaying for a piece, choosing an artwork that doesn't resonate as expected, or misjudging an artist's potential, each mistake provides an opportunity for growth and discovery. Keeping an open mind and viewing mistakes as learning experiences allows collectors to adapt, refine their tastes, and evolve alongside their collections. Additionally, the dynamic nature of the art market means that what may initially seem like a misstep could ultimately result in a rewarding outcome, whether through a shift in personal preferences or a rise in the artist's stature over time

Embracing the Future of Art Acquisition

As you bid farewell to this guide and set sail for new horizons, embrace the boundless possibilities that await in the ever-evolving landscape of art acquisition. Embrace the power of technology to connect, inspire, and transform the way we experience and appreciate art. From virtual reality exhibitions to blockchain-powered marketplaces, the future of art acquisition is limited only by our imagination.

But amidst the dizzying array of technological innovations and digital disruptions, never forget the essence of what makes art collecting truly meaningful: the human connection, the emotional resonance, the shared experience of beauty and wonder. Embrace the joy of discovery, the thrill of acquisition, and the enduring legacy of creativity that transcends time and space.

Conclusion

As we bid adieu to this guide and embark on the next chapter of our artistic odyssey, let us carry with us the lessons learned, the memories cherished, and the dreams yet to be fulfilled. Let us continue to explore, to discover, to create, and to inspire, knowing that the journey is as important as the destination, and that the true value of art lies not in its price tag, but in the joy and meaning it brings to our lives.

So, farewell for now, dear reader, and may your artistic odyssey be filled with laughter, love, and the boundless beauty of the human spirit. And remember, as you navigate the turbulent waters of the art world, always keep your compass pointed true, your sails unfurled, and your heart open to the infinite possibilities that lie ahead.

Bon voyage, dear friend, and may the winds of creativity carry you to wondrous new shores.

Arts are a reflection of our society. In some cases, they can shape our society and is the highest form of hope.—Plato

Appendices

1st Appendix: Glossary of Terms

Decoding the Art World

Welcome to the appendix—a treasure trove of knowledge designed to decode the cryptic language of the art world and illuminate the murky depths of online art buying. Whether you're a seasoned collector or a curious novice, this glossary of terms will guide you through the labyrinth of art jargon with wit, wisdom, and a healthy dose of humor. So, without further ado, let's dive into the alphabet soup of art lingo and emerge enlightened and entertained.

Artisanalisme—*Definition*: The trend of artists marketing their works as authentic and artisanal while mass-producing them in studios or factories. *Example*: Despite claiming to handcraft each piece, Sophie's pottery studio relies on assembly-line production to meet demand.

Artiste Auto-proclamé—*Definition*: A self-proclaimed artist who asserts their artistic status without significant recognition or validation from the art community. *Example*: Despite lacking formal training or exhibition history, Pierre declares himself an artist and begins selling his amateur paintings online.

Artpocalypse—*Definition*: The perceived saturation of the art market with mediocre and derivative works, signaling the decline of meaningful artistic innovation. *Example*: Critics lament the proliferation of uninspired installations and derivative sculptures, bemoaning the impending "artpocalypse."

Auction Snipe—*Definition*: A strategic maneuver in which a bidder swoops in at the last possible moment to place a winning bid, catching competitors off guard and securing the artwork with ninja-like precision. *Example*: "I thought I had the winning bid, but then someone pulled off an auction snipe and stole the artwork right out from under me!"

Bling Bling Art—*Definition*: Ostentatious and flashy artworks that prioritize spectacle over substance, often associated with the excesses of the contemporary art market. *Example*: A gaudy sculpture encrusted with rhinestones and gold leaf draws attention for its extravagance rather than its artistic merit.

Cocktail Vernissage—*Definition*: Art exhibition openings characterized more by socializing and networking opportunities than genuine appreciation of art. *Example*: Attendees at the gallery opening spend more time sipping champagne and mingling than engaging with the artworks on display.

Cryptocurrency Canvas—*Definition*: A cutting-edge platform for buying and selling artworks using cryptocurrency, where blockchain meets brushstroke in a digital dance of commerce and creativity. *Example*: "I just bought a Banksy with Bitcoin on the Cryptocurrency Canvas—it's like art collecting for the digital age!"

Critique d'Art en Carton—*Definition*: Superficial or insincere art criticism lacking depth or insight, often seen in pretenous art reviews or gallery press releases. *Example*: A gallery's press release praises a pile of cardboard boxes as a profound exploration of consumer culture, earning derision from discerning critics.

Dollar Dilemma—*Definition*: The existential crisis that occurs when a bidder's paddle hand trembles uncontrollably at the sight of a seven-figure price tag, prompting a frantic internal debate over the value of art versus the contents of one's bank account. *Example*: "I was all set to bid on that Warhol, but then I had a dollar dilemma and ended up spending the entire auction hiding in the restroom."

Ephemeral Elegance—*Definition*: The fleeting beauty of an artwork that transcends time and space, captivating the viewer's imagination and leaving a lasting impression long after the brushstrokes have faded and the pixels have dissolved into the digital ether. *Example*: "The artist's use of light and shadow imbues the artwork with an ephemeral elegance that transports the viewer to a realm of pure aesthetic bliss."

Forgery Fandango—*Definition*: A high-stakes dance of deception in which a cunning con artist attempts to pass off a counterfeit artwork as the genuine article, leading unwitting buyers on a merry chase through a maze of lies, half-truths, and red herrings. *Example*: "I thought I'd scored a Rembrandt, but it turned out to be a forgery fandango worthy of its own true crime documentary."

Fric Fric Art—*Definition*: Art primarily motivated by financial gain, with little regard for artistic expr ession or cultural significance. *Example*: The artist churns out generic landscape paintings to meet market demand, prioritizing profit over creativity.

Galerie à la Mode—*Definition*: Galleries that prioritize trends and marketability over artistic integrity, featuring works that cater to popular tastes. *Example*: A gallery in a trendy district exclusively exhibits paintings of cats wearing sunglasses, capitalizing on the latest Instagram aesthetic.

Gavel Gravitas—*Definition*: The weighty authority and solemnity bestowed upon a humble wooden gavel as it descends upon the auction block, transforming it from a simple hammer into a symbol of power, prestige, and the almighty dollar. *Example*: "The auctioneer's gavel descended with all the gavel gravitas of a judge delivering a verdict, sealing the fate of the artwork with a resounding thud."

Galerie Éphémère—*Definition*: Temporary exhibition spaces that pop up sporadically, often in trendy neighborhoods, showcasing artworks of questionable quality. *Example*: A vacant storefront transforms into a pop-up gallery overnight, featuring hastily arranged artworks by unknown artists.

Pixel Picassofication—*Definition*: The digital alchemy by which a humble photograph is transformed into a work of art through the magic of Photoshop, turning mundane pixels into masterful brushstrokes and mundane selfies into modern-day masterpieces. *Example*: "With a few clicks of the mouse, I transformed my vacation photos into pixel Picassofications worthy of hanging in the Louvre—or at least my living room."

Prix Gonflé—*Definition*: Artworks with exorbitant price tags, often disproportionate to their artistic merit. *Example*: The gallery lists a small, unremarkable sculpture for €50,000, leading critics to accuse them of inflating prices for profit.

Sticker Shock Syndrome—*Definition*: The acute psychological condition that occurs when a prospective buyer experiences palpitations, dizziness, and mild nausea upon discovering the exorbitant price tag attached to an artwork, leading to a sudden and involuntary loss of consciousness. *Example*: "I had a severe case of sticker shock syndrome when I saw the price of that Damien Hirst—I woke up three days later in the emergency room with a signed print and a hefty hospital bill."

Whimsical Whirlwind—*Definition*: The whimsical journey of discovery and delight that ensues when a collector immerses themselves in the vibrant world of art, embracing unexpected twists and turns with childlike wonder and curiosity. *Example*: "Entering the art world was like stepping into a whimsical whirlwind, where every gallery visit and auction brought new surprises and enchanting encounters with captivating artworks."

2nd Appendix: Webography for Online Art Market Resources

1 · Artsy
(https://www.artsy.net/)
Artsy is a leading online platform for discovering, buying, and selling art. With a vast collection of artworks from galleries, auctions, and art fairs worldwide, Artsy offers a wealth of resources for both seasoned collectors and first-time buyers.

2 · Saatchi Art
(https://www.saatchiart.com/)
Saatchi Art is an online gallery that connects artists with collectors around the world. Featuring a diverse selection of original artworks, including paintings, sculptures, and photography, Saatchi Art offers a curated experience for art enthusiasts of all levels.

3 · Christie's
(https://www.christies.com/)
Christie's is a renowned auction house with a strong online presence, offering a wide range of fine art, decorative objects, and luxury items for sale. With a history dating back over 250 years, Christie's is a trusted source for collectors seeking high-quality artworks and rare treasures.

4 · Sotheby's
(https://www.sothebys.com/)
Sotheby's is another prestigious auction house that conducts auctions both online and in-person. With a focus on fine art, jewelry, and collectibles, Sotheby's provides access to a global marketplace of exceptional artworks and luxury goods.

5 · Drouot Online
(https://www.drouotonline.com/)
Drouot Online is a leading platform for online auctions, offering a wide range of artworks and collectibles from auction houses across France. With its user-friendly interface and extensive catalog, Drouot Online provides an immersive auction experience for art enthusiasts and collectors worldwide.

6 · Interencheres Online
(https://www.interencheres.com/)
Interencheres Online is a comprehensive online platform that brings together over 200 auction houses from across France. With its diverse selection of artworks, antiques, and collectibles, Interencheres Online offers something for every collector, from seasoned connoisseurs to casual enthusiasts.

7 · Artprice
(https://www.artprice.com/)
Artprice is a leading provider of art market data and analytics, offering insights into pricing trends, auction results, and artist performance. With its vast database of artworks and comprehensive analysis tools, Artprice is a valuable resource for collectors, dealers, and investors.

8 · The Art Newspaper
(https://www.theartnewspaper.com/)
The Art Newspaper is a trusted source of news, analysis, and commentary on the art world. With its in-depth articles, interviews, and reviews, The Art Newspaper provides valuable insights into the latest developments and trends shaping the global art market.

9 · ArtNet
(https://www.artnet.com/)
ArtNet is a comprehensive online platform for buying, selling, and researching art. With its extensive database of artworks, auction results, and market analysis, ArtNet offers valuable resources for collectors, dealers, and art enthusiasts worldwide.

10 · Online Galleries and Artist Websites
Many artists and galleries have their own websites and online galleries where they showcase and sell their artwork directly to collectors. Exploring these websites can provide unique insights into artists' work and offer opportunities to purchase directly from the source.

11 · Phillips
(https://www.phillips.com/)
Phillips is a global auction house specializing in contemporary art, modern art, design, and photography. With a focus on emerging and established artists, Phillips offers a dynamic selection of artworks for collectors worldwide.

12 · Bonhams
(https://www.bonhams.com/)
Bonhams is a renowned auction house with a diverse range of departments, including fine art, jewelry, motor cars, and more. With auctions held in locations around the world and an extensive online presence, Bonhams provides access to a wide range of collectible items.

13 · Heritage Auctions
(https://www.ha.com/)
Heritage Auctions is one of the largest auction houses in the world, offering a broad range of collectibles, including fine art, rare books, coins, and sports memorabilia. With its user-friendly website and extensive catalog, Heritage Auctions is a popular choice for collectors and investors.

14 · Artnet Auctions
(https://www.artnet.com/auctions/)
Artnet Auctions is an online platform that hosts auctions featuring a wide range of artworks, from paintings and sculptures to prints and photographs. With its global reach and diverse selection, Artnet Auctions offers opportunities for collectors to acquire works by both established and emerging artists.

15 · Paddle8
(https://www.paddle8.com/)
Paddle8 is an online auction house specializing in contemporary art, design, and collectibles. With its curated selection of artworks and innovative auction formats, Paddle8 offers a dynamic and engaging platform for collectors to discover and acquire unique pieces.

16 · Bukowskis
(https://www.bukowskis.com/)
Bukowskis is a leading auction house based in Sweden, specializing in fine art, antiques, and modern design. With its strong focus on Scandinavian art and design, Bukowskis offers a unique perspective on the international art market.

17 · Koller Auctions
(https://www.kollerauktionen.ch/en/)
Koller Auctions is a Swiss auction house with a diverse range of departments, including fine art, jewelry, watches, and Asian art. With its long-standing reputation for integrity and professionalism, Koller Auctions is a trusted destination for collectors worldwide.

18 · Swann Auction Galleries
(https://www.swanngalleries.com/)
Swann Auction Galleries is a New York-based auction house specializing in rare books, manuscripts, maps, and works on paper. With its focus on historical and culturally significant materials, Swann Auction Galleries offers a unique perspective on the art market.

19 · Freeman's
(https://www.freemansauction.com/)
Freeman's is one of the oldest auction houses in the United States, offering a wide range of fine art, furniture, jewelry, and decorative arts. With its rich history and expertise, Freeman's provides a trusted platform for collectors and sellers alike.

20 · Wright
(https://www.wright20.com/)
Wright is a Chicago-based auction house specializing in modern and contemporary design. With its focus on innovative and iconic works, Wright offers a curated selection of furniture, lighting, and decorative arts for discerning collectors

3rd Appendix: Bibliography

Books

ADAM, Georgina. *Dark Side of the Boom: The Excesses of the Art Market in the 21st Century*. Lund Humphries, 2018.

ADAM, Georgina. *Big Bucks: The Explosion of the Art Market in the 21st Century*. Lund Humphries, 2014.

BECKET, Richard, and Susie Hodge. *How to Sell Art Online: The Expert Guide to Finding Buyers, Getting Noticed, and Making Money*. Watson-Guptill, 2019.

CROW, Kelly. *The Art of the Sale: Learning from the Masters About the Business of Art*. Harper Business, 2017.

DE PURY, Simon. *The Auctioneer: Adventures in the Art Trade*. St. Martin's Press, 2016.

FOWLE, Francesca. *Art Collecting: A Beginner's Guide*. Thames & Hudson, 2020.

HOOK, Philip. *Breakfast at Sotheby's: An A-Z of the Art World*. Penguin Books, 2013.

HOOK, Philip. *Rogues' Gallery: The Rise (and Occasional Fall) of Art Dealers, the Hidden Players in the History of Art*. Profile Books, 2017.

MCANDREW, Clare. *The Art Market 2021: An Art Basel and UBS Report*. Art Basel, 2021.

ROBERTSON, Iain, and DERRICK Chong, eds. *The Art Business*. Routledge, 2008.

THORNTON, Sarah. *Seven Days in the Art World*. W. W. Norton & Company, 2008.

Articles and Reports

Artsy Editorial. *"The Online Art Market: A Comprehensive Overview."* Artsy, 2020.

Deloitte. *"Art & Finance Report 2021."* Deloitte Luxembourg, 2021.

McAndrew, Clare. *"The Art Market 2020."* Art Basel and UBS Report, 2020.

Skate's Art Market Research. *"The Skate's Annual Art Investment Report."* Skate's Art Market Research, 2021.

Websites

Artnet. "Artnet Price Database." Accessed May 15, 2023. www.artnet.com.

Artprice. "Artprice Annual Report: The Art Market in 2021." Accessed April 10, 2023. www.artprice.com.

Artsy. "Buy Art from Leading Galleries and Auctions." Accessed June 1, 2023. www.artsy.net.

Christie's. "Christie's Auction House." Accessed May 20, 2023. www.christies.com.

Drouot Online. "The Online Auction Platform of Drouot." Accessed June 10, 2023. www.drouotonline.com.

Interencheres. "Live Auctions from France." Accessed June 5, 2023. www.interencheres.com.

Saatchi Art. "The World's Leading Online Art Gallery." Accessed May 25, 2023. www.saatchiart.com.

Sotheby's. "Sotheby's Auction House." Accessed May 20, 2023. www.sothebys.com.

Academic Journals

BURTON, Diana. *"Online Art Sales: The Changing Landscape of the Art Market." Journal of Art Market Studies*, vol. 5, no. 2, 2019, pp. 45-60.

SMITH, John. *"The Impact of Digital Platforms on Art Transactions." International Journal of Art & Commerce*, vol. 3, no. 1, 2020, pp. 12-34.

WALKER, Susan. *"From Gallery to Screen: The Evolution of Art Sales in the Digital Age." Art Market Journal*, vol. 2, no. 3, 2018, pp. 88-102.

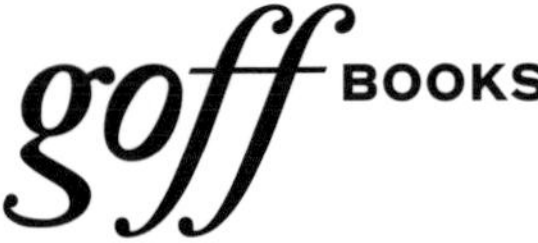

Published by Goff Books
An Imprint of ORO Editions

www.goffbooks.com
info@goffbooks.com

Goff Books makes a continuous effort to minimize the overall carbon footprint of its publications. As part of this goal, Goff Books, in association with Global ReLeaf, arranges to plant trees to replace those used in the manufacturing of the paper produced for its books. Global ReLeaf is an international campaign run by American Forests, one of the world's oldest nonprofit conservation organizations. Global ReLeaf is American Forests' education and action program that helps individuals, organizations, agencies, and corporations improve the local and global environment by planting and caring for trees.

Author
Simone Falanca

Managing Editor
Jake Anderson

Book Design
Tia Džamonja

Prepress & Print work
ORO Editions Inc.

Printing & Binding
China

Publisher
Gordon Goff

10 9 8 7 6 5 4 3 2 1 First Edition

ISBN: 978-1-961856-96-7